This is the second volume in a series
of Finders' Guides to Works in the
Smithsonian Institution. The first
volume is by Lynda Corey Claassen,
*Finders' Guide to Prints and Drawings in
the Smithsonian Institution*, published by
the Smithsonian Institution Press,
Washington, D.C., 1981.

Finders' Guide to

DECORATIVE ARTS

in the Smithsonian Institution

Christine Minter-Dowd

Smithsonian Institution Press
Washington, D.C. 1984

This is the second volume in a series of Finders' Guides to Works in the Smithsonian Institution; the first volume, published in 1981, is *Finders' Guide to Prints and Drawings in the Smithsonian Institution*. ISBN 0–87474–316–8 (cloth)/ ISBN 0–87474–317–6 (pbk)

Volume editor: Jeanne M. Sexton

The paper in this book meets the guidelines for permanence and durability of the Committee on Production Guidelines for Book Longevity of the Council on Library Resources.

Library of Congress Cataloging in Publication Data
Smithsonian Institution.
    Finders' guide to decorative arts in the Smithsonian Institution.
    (Finders' guides to works in the Smithsonian Institution)
    Includes bibliographies and index.
    Supt. of Docs. no.: SI 1.20:D35
    1. Art industries and trade— Washington, D.C.—Guide-books. 2. Decoration and ornament—Washington, D.C.—Guide-books. 3. Smithsonian Institution—Guide-books. I. Minter-Dowd, Christine. II. Title. III. Series: Smithsonian Institution. Finders' guides to works in the Smithsonian Institution.
NK460.W3S67
1984   745'.074'0153   82–600320
ISBN 0–87474–636–1
ISBN 0–87474–637–X (pbk.)

Cover:
Detail, printed cotton, ca. 1800–1810.
Designed by Jean-Baptiste Huet.
Printed by Oberkampf, Jouy-en-Josas, France. Cooper-Hewitt Museum, Department of Decorative Arts.

Frontispiece:
Arm chair, 1847.
Designed by James Renwick for the Regent's Room, Smithsonian Institution Building.
USA.
Walnut with gilt decoration.

CONTENTS

CONTENTS

FOREWORD

In 1979 a Decorative Arts Committee was established at the Smithsonian Institution to define, locate, and enumerate the decorative arts and related collections throughout the diverse museums and bureaux comprising the Institution. The committee was fortunate in securing the professional services of Christine Minter-Dowd, an art historian formerly associated with the Museum of Early Southern Decorative Arts in Winston-Salem, to prepare this volume. She spent three arduous years exploring storerooms, interviewing curators, and inspecting thousands of objects and records in a multitude of media, shapes, and sizes from both domestic and foreign cultures. Among the many major collections she studied was that of anthropology—hitherto thought of only in scientific terms.

The resulting comprehensive publication, *Finders' Guide to Decorative Arts in the Smithsonian Institution* is the first of its type to appear for an American museum. It will serve as a model others might follow. The wide range of collections of decorative arts within the Smithsonian complex have, for the first time, been carefully defined and indexed, to provide accessibility for both American and foreign scholars. In recent years the growth of the Smithsonian collections has made it impossible for any one curator to know the location or scope of decorative arts in other Smithsonian sister museums. For instance, one would hardly have been aware until now that one of the principal collections of eighteenth century French furniture in Washington is located in the Smithsonian's National Air and Space Museum! This collection, on public display, consists of furnishings designed and decorated with balloon motifs—all illustrating the invention and tremendous popularity of the new hot air balloon in Paris in the 1790s.

This book is the second in a series of Finders' Guides to the Smithsonian collections recommended for publication by the Smithsonian Council in 1976. The *Finders' Guide to Prints and Drawings in the Smithsonian Institution* by Lynda Corey Claassen has enjoyed considerable success since its publication by the Smithsonian Institution Press in 1981. That publication, as well as this one, provides the scholar with vital information on each collection, including the loan policy, public access, and photoduplication service. In addition, all objects are cross-indexed by media, period, and style in order to provide additional invaluable research aid for the decorative arts historian.

S. DILLON RIPLEY
Secretary, Smithsonian Institution

ACKNOWLEDGMENTS

Hundreds of staff members of the Smithsonian Institution helped to make this *Guide* possible. Their contributions were varied, ranging from describing collections, leading me through vast storage areas, reading and revising collection descriptions, providing custom-made computer-generated lists, and last but of monumental importance, typing portions of the manuscript.

Several people have made major contributions to this publication. The seven members of the Smithsonian Institution Decorative Arts Committee acted as my advisors during the entire project. In addition, they initiated contact between the author and the various bureaus, read numerous drafts, as well as the completed manuscript, and were always available for inspiration and counseling: Anne C. Golovin, National Museum of American History, James M. Goode, Smithsonian Institution Building, Susan A. Hamilton, Archives of American Art, Lloyd E. Herman, Renwick Gallery of the National Museum of American Art, David R. McFadden, Cooper-Hewitt Museum, and U. Vincent Wilcox, Museum Support Center. From the Office of Computer Services, James J. Crockett, Deputy Director, and Penelope A. Packard, Systems Analyst, supervised the computerization of the Location Guide to Artists, Designers, Makers, Manufacturers, Production Centers, and Retailers. Ruth W. Spiegel, a senior editor at the Smithsonian Institution Press, developed the clear and useable format from a mass of complex material. My sincerest and warmest thanks to Jeanne Sexton, the volume editor. Her expertise brought clarity and comfort to an author inexperienced in the process of book production.

LIST OF ILLUSTRATIONS

INTRODUCTION

The Smithsonian Institution is a collection of museums and research organizations encompassing a wide range of subject areas and collecting philosophies. The purpose of the *Finders' Guide to Decorative Arts in the Smithsonian Institution* is to introduce researchers to the vast collections of decorative arts and to the complex organizational structure of the Smithsonian. The *Guide* is a brief survey of the collections which indicates the access routes available to researchers wishing to study holdings in the national museums.

The scope of this reference book is more inclusive than the title implies. The term decorative arts is commonly applied to three-dimensional utilitarian objects with aesthetic merit. The *Guide* encompasses these anticipated forms, but it additionally includes material which, although it may not be normally classified as such, can relate to the study of decorative arts. Collections of archeological, ethnological, and technological artifacts are within the purview of this survey. These associated collections add an interdisciplinary dimension to the study of decorative arts as traditionally defined.

Forms and techniques which have been excluded from the *Guide* are painting, printmaking, drawing, photography, and sculpture.

Preparation of the Guide

The *Finders' Guide to Decorative Arts in the Smithsonian Institution* contains information gathered between June 1979 and December 1981. This survey was performed with the assistance of staff members familiar with the collections—directors, curators, collection managers, specialists, inventory personnel, archivists, and librarians. The survey included general inquiries regarding the collection; examination of existing finding aids and publications; and, in some cases, the review of entire collections or portions of collections.

Manuscript drafts were approved by collection curators or unit heads, and the museums' directors.

Organization of the Guide

The *Guide* is arranged alphabetically by the name of the museum or other office. Within each museum, the collections, departments, or divisions are also arranged alphabetically. Each museum or other office is assigned a number, and each subunit is assigned a number-letter designation. For example, the Cooper-Hewitt Museum is designated 2; its Department of Decorative Arts is 2A. These alphanumeric identifications have been used in indexing the volume.

DESCRIPTIVE STATEMENT

There is a general statement about the research and collecting objectives of each Smithsonian Institution museum or office, as well as information about when it was established and the building in which it is housed. The description of each unit, department, or division within the museums or offices, contains a statement of general purpose, scope, and approximate count of the collection. Collection strengths according to object types, geographic origin, and date are noted, and when possible, items of extraordinary quality, quantity, or interest are mentioned.

Consistency has been a principal goal throughout the preparation of this volume. Apparent inconsistencies in the information contained in the *Guide* reflect the different purposes of collections and the variations in the information available to the researcher within the units.

SYSTEM FOR CLASSIFICATION OF OBJECTS

In order to condense a large amount of information into a reasonable space, and to facilitate the use of the *Guide*, objects have been classified according to the principles of *function* and/or *material*. Classification headings are listed below with explanations as necessary.

Architectural elements—including models
Arms and armor—including accessories for firearms
Basketry
Bibelots and miniatures—excluding models
Ceramics
Costume (garments and accessories)
Enamel
Furniture
Glass
Heating devices
Jewelry
Lacquer
Lighting devices
Machinery and tools—including items with decorative elements
Metalwork: Base metals
Metalwork: Precious metals
Musical instruments
Textiles—including woven and nonwoven fiber items
Timepieces and measuring devices
Toys and games
Wallpaper

Other materials
  Bone
  Horn

Ivory
Jade
Leather
Stone
Wood

Users of the *Guide* looking for a particular object type or material should read all possible pertinent classification headings since various curatorial units study and classify material in different ways. For example, a watch may be classified variously: in the Cooper-Hewitt Museum's Department of Decorative Arts, a watch in the form of a brooch may be classified under Jewelry; in the National Museum of American History, Division of Transportation, a pocket watch may be classified under Timepieces and Measuring Devices.

The format for the classified entries is as follows: number of objects, object name, material, place of origin, and date of production. Entries include all of this information and in this order whenever possible. Variations reflect differing information available in the respective units.

Number of objects.
Since the number of accessioned objects in a given collection is constantly changing, all totals are approximate. "Small collection" refers to a group of less than twenty-five objects.

Object name.
Selected generic terms have been used throughout the text (e.g., furniture, tablewares, vessels). Titles of works are in italics.

Material.
Major materials are listed alphabetically.

Place of origin.
References may be to a cultural area, region, country, or continent. Inconsistencies in place names reflect the usage of the curatorial unit. For example, the terms Iran, Persia, Near East, Middle East, and Asia are used by various units to refer to the same area. Place names are listed alphabetically.

Date of production.
Inclusive dates are generally stated in centuries. Terms designating style are not used.

SELECTED PUBLICATIONS
Selected books, exhibition catalogs, periodicals, and journal articles which describe and illustrate a significant number of decorative arts from the collections are listed at the end of the appropriate unit.

LENDING POLICY
The Smithsonian Institution attempts to make its collections available for museum exhibitions and other scholarly purposes. Each museum or office has its own lending policy and considers each request individually. Consequently, procedures for borrowing vary, and in some cases, restrictions prohibit any lending. All requests must be in writing, well in advance. Information regarding to whom

loan inquiries should be addressed has been included after every unit description.

FINDING AIDS

Card catalogs, indexes, and inventories that provide information about the collections have been described. These finding aids are available in the respective unit, and each reflects that unit's system for organizing records of objects or the objects themselves (e.g., by subject, culture, origin, material).

PHOTODUPLICATION SERVICE

Unless restricted for specific reasons, photographs of objects in the collection may be available to researchers. All requests must include the negative or slide number, which may be obtained from the appropriate curatorial unit. Not all collection materials are available currently as photographs; should photography be required for objects not previously photographed, special fees may be involved to cover the costs. Requests for photographs should be directed to the appropriate curatorial unit which will provide all pertinent information. Prepayment is generally required.

Researchers must have written permission of the appropriate unit to reproduce any Smithsonian Institution photographs.

PUBLIC ACCESS

All requests for information should be written and stated as specifically as possible. Correspondence should be addressed to the museum or office best equipped to respond.

Appointments are required to visit any collection not on public view. Written requests for appointments should explain the purpose and scope of the research project and should be addressed to the appropriate office. Appointments may be scheduled between 10 A.M. and 5 P.M., Monday through Friday.

All museums in Washington, D.C., except the National Museum of African Art, are open to the public from 10 A.M. to 5:30 P.M. every day except Christmas Day. Some museums on the Mall are open until 9 P.M. during the summer.

The National Museum of African Art, which is located on Capitol Hill, is open from 11 A.M. to 5 P.M. daily except Christmas Day, noon to 5 P.M. on weekends. Museum hours may be extended between Memorial Day and Labor Day.

Visiting hours at the Cooper-Hewitt Museum in New York City are as follows: closed Monday, open Tuesday 10 A.M. to 9 P.M., Wednesday through Saturday 10 A.M. to 5 P.M., Sunday noon to 5 P.M.

The Smithsonian Institution does not give appraisals of objects or collections. If requested, the museums or offices may be able to provide, without recommendations, names of appraisers or organizations of appraisers.

Index

The Index is intended to provide access to the information in this *Guide*. It is a single, letter-by-letter alphabetical list that includes the following terms drawn from the text:

personal names
names of authors in the bibliographic entries
geographic and corporate names
titles of works
materials (e.g., aluminium, glass, textiles)
headings from the classification list
object types (e.g., mirrors, tiles, uniforms)
subjects (e.g., engineering, ethnology)

Index headings are used as direct headings and frequently as subheadings.

References are only to the alphanumeric unit designations; page numbers are never used. The Index should be used in conjunction with the Location Guide to Artists, Designers, Makers, Manufacturers, Production Centers, and Retailers. While the Location Guide lists these names which are represented in eight major collections of decorative arts, the Index may provide additional locations by directing the user to collection descriptions which mention the identical name. For example, a researcher wishing to know which collections of the Smithsonian Institution contain works by Mary Chase Perry may consult only the Location Guide; the location listed is 8B. The Index, however, directs researchers to two additional locations, 1, 3A, and also describes the context in which these objects are held.

Location Guide to Artists, Designers, Makers, Manufacturers, Production Centers, and Retailers

The Location Guide to Artists, Designers, Makers, Manufacturers, Production Centers, and Retailers is a computer-generated listing of all such names related to the decorative arts in eight major collections of decorative arts in the Smithsonian Institution:

Cooper-Hewitt Museum
    Department of Decorative Arts and
    Department of Wallpaper
National Museum of American Art
National Museum of American History
    Division of Ceramics and Glass
    Division of Community Life
    Division of Costume
    Division of Domestic Life
    Division of Musical Instruments
    Division of Textiles

Proper names in the Location Guide were compiled from files of the units listed above. Every effort was made to standardize the spelling of these names and the alphabetical ordering of names with articles (e.g., de, le, la). Diacritical marks do not appear because of limitations imposed by the computer.

The Location Guide identifies the collection in which the name is recorded. It is not an index to the text of this volume.

THE COLLECTIONS

1

Archives of American Art

The Archives of American Art is a research facility committed to stimulating and aiding scholarship in American art. It acquires and preserves the correspondence, diaries, sketch books, business records, and photographs of artists, critics, dealers, and collectors, as well as the official records of galleries, museums, and art organizations. Among the craftsmen, designers, and organizations whose papers are in these collections are Anni Albers, Clayton Bailey, Kenneth Francis Bates, Black Mountain College, Detroit Society of Arts and Crafts, Kenneth Ferguson, Dominick Labino, the League of New Hampshire Craftsmen, Dorothy Liebes, Harvey Littleton, Ronald H. Pearson, Adelaide Alsop Robineau, Terrance Robsjohn-Gibbings, Viktor Schreckengost, Arthur Stone, Mary Chase Stratton (Pewabic Pottery), Richard Thomas, Marguerite Wildenhain, Margaret Craver Withers, Jan Yoors, and Claire Zeisler.

In order to preserve the contents of the original documents and make them easily accessible to the greatest number of researchers, microfilm copies and finding aids are maintained at each of the regional centers in Boston, New York,

1 Working drawing.
 Ink on tracing paper.
 Arthur J. Stone Papers (b. 1847–d.1938).

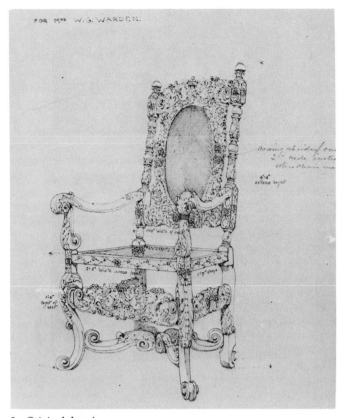

2 Original drawing.
Pencil on paper.
Irving and Casson Papers, 1910–60.

Washington, D.C., Detroit, and San Francisco. The microfilm is also available through interlibrary loan.

SELECTED PUBLICATIONS

Breton, Arthur J.; Zembala, Nancy H.; and Nicastro, Anne P., comps. *Archives of American Art: A Checklist of the Collection*. Washington, D.C.: Archives of American Art, 1975, 1977, 1978.

Checklist of all collections acquired to 1978.

McCoy, Garnett. *Archives of American Art: A Directory of Resources*. New York: R. R. Bowker and Co., 1972.

Lists and briefly describes 555 collections which total approximately 2 million items.

The Archives of American Art Journal. 1 –. 1960 –. New York.

This quarterly publication contains articles based on the Archives' holdings.

3 Photographs of stencils.
Janet Waring Papers, ca. 1932.

Also included are reports on the collecting activities of the regional centers, new acquisitions, and descriptions of recently cataloged collections.

The Card Catalog of the Manuscript Collections of the Archives of American Art. 10 vols. Wilmington, Del.: Scholarly Resources Inc., 1980.

PUBLIC ACCESS

The Archives of American Art is located at the following addresses. Researchers should contact specific office for hours.

Boston:	86 Mount Vernon Street, Boston, Massachusetts 02108
Detroit:	5200 Woodward Avenue, Detroit, Michigan 48202
New York:	41 East 65th Street, New York, New York 10021
San Francisco:	M. H. deYoung Memorial Museum, Golden Gate Park, San Francisco, California 94118
Washington, D.C.:	8th and F Streets, N.W., Washington, D.C. 20560

2

Cooper-Hewitt Museum
Smithsonian Institution's National Museum of Design

Peter Cooper, inventor and philanthropist, established the Cooper Union for the advancement of Science and Art in 1859. This tuition-free coeducational school provided instruction in design, engineering, and other technical subjects.

Peter Cooper's granddaughters, Sarah, Eleanor, and Amy Hewitt, carried out a plan of Cooper's, never realized in his own lifetime, when they established the Cooper Union Museum for the Arts of Decoration in 1897. From the outset, the Museum's collection was intended to be a comprehensive survey of design

4   Bandbox with cover, ca. 1830.
    USA.
    Printed paper on cardboard.

with a strong emphasis on European decorative arts. Objects were acquired to illustrate educational and historical themes, to provide enjoyment and opportunity for research, to represent most major periods and styles, and to serve as a resource for students of design.

In 1963, due to economic factors, the trustees of the Cooper Union were faced with closing the Museum and dispersing the collection. A committee was formed to maintain the Museum and to preserve its cohesive collections. The Cooper Union Museum for the Arts of Decoration became the Cooper-Hewitt Museum and in 1968, a part of the Smithsonian Institution. In 1970, the collections were moved into the Carnegie Mansion, which was later restored and renovated. In 1976, the Museum opened to the public in its new facility.

The Cooper-Hewitt is composed of the Department of Drawings and Prints, the Department of Textiles, the Department of Wallpaper, and the Department of Decorative Arts. The purpose of the Museum—to serve the professional de-

5   Desk, ca. 1905.
    Designed by Carlo Zen, Milan, Italy.
    Wood, inlaid with brass and mother-of-
    pearl.

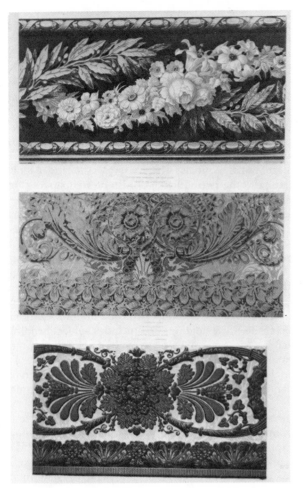

6   Wallpaper, ca. 1820.
     France.
     Printed from woodblocks.

sign community—has remained the same since its inception. In addition, the Museum now serves a large general public as well as specialized students. The Drawings and Prints collection numbers more than 100,000 items. Holdings rank among the finest in unique folios and comprehensive groups of graphic material. Within the collections are several thousand European designs for architecture, costume, decoration, and textiles; ornament prints; and wood engravings. For a complete description of the holdings of the Department, see the *Finders' Guide to Prints and Drawings in the Smithsonian Institution* by Lynda C. Claassen.

The Cooper-Hewitt Library is a readily accessible reference collection of design and decorative arts. A collection of rare books includes volumes on 17th-

and 18th-century architecture, early natural history books, and books of festival decorations. The reference library collection contains catalogs of exhibitions and international expositions, catalogs from major auction houses in England and America, and hand-colored fashion plates.

There are five collections of special note in the Library's holdings. The Color Archive contains book material and color samples used in the fashion industry from 1896 to 1970. The Donald Deskey Archive is comprised of materials relating to his career (late 1920s–'60s) as both an industrial and interior designer and includes designs for the interior of Radio City Music Hall. The Henry Dreyfus Archive encompasses his theatrical and industrial design materials as well as his work developing international symbols. The Nancy McClelland Archive contains information relating to the reproduction of historic wallpapers along with her research and lecture notes concerning the New York City cabinetmaker Duncan Phyfe. The Ladislav Sutner Archive contains graphic and advertising materials from the 1940s to 1974. For a complete description of the Cooper-Hewitt Library's collections, see the *Finders' Guide to Prints and Drawings*.

The Cooper-Hewitt Museum Library Picture Collection is a separate but related part of the Museum Library. More than 1½ million illustrations from books and periodicals, as well as many trade catalogs, are organized by subject and century. The purpose of this pictorial collection is to provide images and information related to aspects of the decorative arts and design. An index of the collection provides access to these holdings and includes subject headings such as: Animals, Architecture, Arms and Armor, Ceramics, Costume, Countries and People, Dance, Decoration and Ornament, House and Home (Home Furnishings, Cleaning Materials and Products, Linens), Interiors (of Hotels, Private Residences, Trains), Religious Furnishings, Tapestries, and Sports—to name only a few.

The Thérèse Bonney Collection of photographs dating from 1925 to 1939 are of special interest. Bonney, who lived in Paris, was a commercial photographer and offered a subscription service to designers, decorators, and manufacturers of the most recent works of French designers. These promotional photographs include domestic and commercial interiors, beauty salons, restaurants, and a variety of commercial products.

SELECTED PUBLICATIONS

An American Museum of Decorative Art and Design: Designs from the Cooper-Hewitt Collection, New York. London: Arts Council of Great Britain, 1973.

This exhibition catalog contains descriptions and illustrations of 33 bandboxes, textiles, and wallpapers from the Museum's collection.

The Cooper Union Museum Chronicles. New York: Cooper Union Museum. Volumes published 1935 to 1963.

The *Chronicles* contain scholarly essays about the Museum's collections. Monographs pertain to a variety of decorative arts holdings including gilt bronze furniture mounts, ceramics, Japanese sword mounts, textiles, tiles, wallpaper, and recent gifts to the Museum. In general, publication was annual, with some irregularities during later years. Indexed only through 1958.

Gilchrist, Brenda, gen. ed. *The Smithsonian Illustrated Library of Antiques*. New

York: Cooper-Hewitt Museum, 1979.

Each volume in this series surveys the history of a specific form—clocks, furniture, glass, jewelry, needlework, oriental rugs, porcelain, pottery, prints, silver, and toys and games. Books are written by experts in the field and contain illustrations of many pieces in the Cooper-Hewitt Museum and the National Museum of American History.

An Illustrated Survey of the Collections. New York: Cooper Union Museum, 1957.

This catalog illustrates and describes 39 objects from the collection. Forms include ceramics, furniture, glass, Japanese sword mounts and other metal work, textiles, and wallpaper.

Lynes, Russell. *More Than Meets the Eye: The History and Collections of Cooper-Hewitt Museum.* Introduction by Mary A. Noon. New York: Cooper-Hewitt Museum, 1981.

This volume provides a comprehensive history of the Cooper-Hewitt Museum from the time of its founding in 1897 to the present day. Collections of each of the curatorial departments—Decorative Arts, Prints and Drawings, Wallpaper, and Textiles—are thoroughly described. Unique objects are highlighted; 249 illustrations.

Reau, Louis. *The Four Continents: From the Collection of James Hazen Hyde.* New York: Cooper Union Museum, 1961.

This exhibition catalog includes ceramics, graphics, glass, metalwork, textiles, and other materials illustrating the allegory of the Four Continents—Europe, Asia, the Americas, and Africa.

Recent Acquisitions by the Cooper Union Museum. New York: Cooper Union Museum, 1964.

Ceramics, furniture, glass, jewelry, metalwork, textiles, and wallpapers are described and illustrated.

2A

Department of Decorative Arts

The collections of the Department of Decorative Arts document major trends of design and style. Holdings number approximately 14,000 objects, with particular strength in metalwork, ceramics, glass, and furniture from the post-Renaissance period to the present. Also, within the collection are representative examples of ancient and classical artifacts, and Asian and American objects pertinent to the study of design. Both unique handcrafted objects as well as multiple and mass-produced items are included in these holdings.

The collection of silver is strongest in European objects made from the 17th through the 20th centuries. English, French, German, and Scandinavian tablewares and decorative objects are particularly significant and diverse. Notable wares include a silver teakettle on stand with spirit lamp, by William Fawdery, London, 1711–12, an urn by Thomas Heming of London, 1777–78, a silver gilt jug by Joseph Angell III, also of London, 1854–55, a bowl by Josef Hoffmann from the Weiner Werkstaette, 1917, and a 17th-century Augsburg charger by Adolf Gaap.

The largest single collection of metalwork is the Carol B. Brener and Stephen W. Brener Collection of more than 4,000 matchsafes. This collection documents the history of popular styles from the mid-19th to early 20th centuries in a variety of metals and other mixed materials.

Japanese metalworking techniques and materials are illustrated in the George Cameron Stone Collection of 1,200 sword fittings. Most of the important techniques and schools of *tsuba* (sword guard) makers from the 12th to the 19th centuries are represented. In addition to *tsuba*, *fuchi*, *kashira*, *kozuka*, and *menuki* are also included. Most examples were collected for their importance as records of metallurgical techniques and alloys.

Hardware of a different nature is represented in the Department's collection of European gilt bronze and brass furniture mounts. The important Léon Decloux collection of 18th- and early 19th-century French metalwork includes hundreds of these furniture mounts.

The ceramics collection encompasses earthenware, stoneware, and porcelain from Europe, the classical Mediterranean area, the Americas, Asia, and North Africa. The largest portion of the collection provides an overview of European ceramics from the 17th through 20th centuries.

Important porcelain factories such as Chelsea, Meissen, and Sèvres are well represented, along with 17th- and 18th-century faïence, delftware, and art pottery from the 19th and 20th centuries. The Mrs. John Jay Ide Collection of 18th-century French soft paste porcelain contains mostly Sèvres pieces. The Museum's collection also holds rare examples of the original designs for 18th-century porcelains and in some cases, the drawings have been joined with the actual objects of identical design.

Ceramics of special interest made by 19th- and 20th-century artists include a plate by the French artist-potter Joseph-Théodore Deck, ca. 1870, a punchbowl by the American ceramist Viktor Schreckengost, ca. 1929, a table service by Russel Wright, known for his innovative industrial design, works by Émile Gallé, Rookwood pottery, and examples by 20th-century artist-potters.

The Department's furniture collection contains primarily European pieces from the 17th through the 20th centuries. Works by important American, English, and French craftsmen, designers, and manufacturers constitute a major portion of these holdings. Notable designers and craftsmen represented in the collection include Jules Dessoir, Jean Dunand, Charles Eames, Jean-Michel Frank, Terrence Robsjohn-Gibbings, Hector Guimard, Josef Hoffmann, Louis Majorelle, David Roentgen, and Frank Lloyd Wright. Special materials and techniques are also illustrated such as papier-mâché, marquetry, and various lacquer techniques.

Several of the Department's collections contain a variety of materials and forms. The James Hazen Hyde Collection encompasses allegorical and symbolic representations of the Four Continents—Europe, Asia, Africa, and the Americas—as depicted in European decorative arts of the 17th through 19th centuries. This theme is represented in figures, plaques, glass, silver, woodwork, glyptic arts, and textiles.

Another important group of objects made of various materials is Mrs. J. Insley Blair's collection of American lighting devices. Forms include betty lamps, grease lamps, and rush holders made and used during the 18th and 19th centuries.

From the collection of the late Stanley Siegel, the gift of Stanley Siegel, there are ceramics by Edouard-Marcel Sandoz, glass by René Lalique and Louis Comfort Tiffany, and metalwork by Edgar Brandt, along with other decorative arts from the 1900–30 period.

The Susan Dwight Bliss Collection includes bibelots, boxes, keys and locks, and jewelry.

A unique collection of 18th- and 19th-century Swiss decorative arts, most with folk motifs, was given to the Museum by the descendents of the collectors, C. Helme and Alice B. Strater. Materials include ceramics, glass, metalwork, and woodwork.

Holdings of puppetry items include the extensive Frank and Elizabeth Haines gift of marionettes used by both of them in the 20th century, and a rare group of 18th-century Venetian *commedia dell' arte* figures.

CLASSIFIED CATALOG OF OBJECTS

Architectural Elements
300 architectural elements and models; ceramic, iron, marble, wood; Austria, Bohemia, Egypt, England, France, Germany, India, Italy, Netherlands, Russia, Spain, Siam, Sweden, USA; 4th through 20th centuries (primarily 18th-century French).

Bibelots and Miniatures
100 boxes (including betel nut, bride's, insect, match, patch, sewing, snuff, tobacco), étuis, and nécessaires; enamel, lacquer, leather, papier-mâché, wood, precious metals and stones; Austria, Bhutan, China, England, Egypt, France, Germany, India, Iran, Italy, Japan, Netherlands, North Africa, Norway, Philippines, Russia, Santo Domingo, Spain, Switzerland, USA; 16th through 20th centuries (primarily 18th-century French).
30 *inrō* and *netsuke*; agate, bone, cloisonné enamel, ebony, ivory, lacquer, papier-mâché, wood; Japan; 18th through 20th centuries.
4,200 matchsafes; brass, bronze, ceramics, copper, enamel, gold, ivory, silver, synthetics, tin, wood; England, France, Japan, USA; 1850–1925.

Ceramics
small reference collection of earthenware and stoneware incense burners, tomb figures, vessels; China; 1st through 15th centuries.
125 earthenware figures, fragments, lamps, vessels; Egypt, Iran, Turkey, Greece; 16th century B.C. through 5th century A.D.
small reference collection of earthenware fragments, vessels; Middle and South America; 18th through 20th centuries.
400 tiles (including floor, stove, wall tiles); Austria, England, France, Germany, India, Iran, Italy, Netherlands, Portugal, Spain, Sweden, Turkey, USA; 13th

through 20th centuries.

20 earthenware lamps and pipe bowls; North Africa; 18th and 19th centuries.

1,000 earthenware, stoneware, and porcelain objects (including boxes, decorative pieces, figures, garden ornaments, plaques, tablewares); Austria, Belgium, Denmark, England, Finland, France, Germany, Ireland, Italy, Iran, Mexico, Netherlands, Russia, Spain, Sweden, Switzerland, USA; 16th through 20th centuries.

225 earthenware, stoneware, and porcelain figures, snuff bottles, tewares, vessels, writing equipment; China, Japan, Korea; 17th through 20th centuries.

Costumes (Garments and Accessories)

3,500 buttons and two button sample books; bone, brass, celluloid, crystal, glass, gold, ivory, pearl, steel, wood, precious and nonprecious metals and stones; China, England, France, Haiti, Iran, Russia, USA; 18th through 20th centuries.

Enamel

50 enamel clocks, lighting devices, plaques, tablewares; Austria, England, France, Germany, Norway, Iran, Russia, Spain, Sweden, Switzerland, USA; 16th through 20th centuries.

25 enamel boxes, cases, incense burners, tewares; China, Japan; 18th through 20th centuries.

Furniture and Woodcarvings

400 pieces of furniture (primarily chairs); bamboo, glass, lacquer, metal, papier-mâché, plastic, wood; Austria, Canada, China, Denmark, Dutch East Indies, England, Finland, France, Germany, Greece, Iran, Ireland, Italy, Japan, Netherlands, Spain, Sweden, USA; 15th through 20th centuries (primarily English and French, wood and metal, 18th and 20th centuries).

50 wooden boxes, desk items, ornaments, smoking equipment, woodenwares; Bhutan, China, Costa Rica, Denmark, Egypt, England, France, Germany, Italy, Japan, Java, Netherlands, Iran, Sweden, Switzerland, USA; 17th through 20th centuries.

small collection of bird cages; ceramics, enamel, glass, horn, lacquer, silver, steel, tortoise shell, wire, wood; China, England, France, Holland, Italy, Japan, Spain, USA; 17th through 20th centuries.

Glass

65 ancient glass fragments and vessels; Egypt, Greece, Iran, Syria; 1st century B.C. through 10th century A.D.

400 glass objects (including chandeliers, clocks, decorative pieces, jewelry, snuffboxes, tablewares); Austria, Bohemia, China, Czechoslovakia, England, Finland, France, Germany, Ireland, Italy, Japan, Netherlands, Silesia, Sweden, Switzerland, USA; 16th through 20th centuries.

Jewelry

500 pieces of jewelry (collected for their design rather than for their inherent value in precious materials); aluminium, amber, base metals, ceramic, coral, enamel, glass, hair, ivory, jade, jet, pinchbeck, precious metals and stones,

tortoiseshell; Austria, Africa, Bhutan, Brazil, Central America, China, Denmark, East Indies, England, France, Germany, Sweden, India, Italy, Japan, Mexico, Netherlands, Norway, Panama, Philippines, Russia, Scotland, Spain, Switzerland, Thailand, Turkey, USA (primarily England, France, Italy, USA); 18th through 20th centuries.

Lacquer
25 lacquer architectural elements, boxes, screens, tewares, writing implements; China, France, Germany, Japan, Indonesia, Iran, Siam; 17th through 20th centuries.

Lighting Devices
small reference collection of ancient lighting devices; earthenware; Iran, Mesopotamia; 6th century B.C. through 13th century A.D.
100 lighting devices (including candlesticks, candelabra, chandeliers, sconces, lanterns); brass, bronze, enamel, glass, iron, marble, pewter, porcelain, quillwork, silver, tin, tôle; Belgium, China, Czechoslovakia, England, France, Germany, India, Ireland, Italy, Netherlands, North Africa, Iran, Spain (primarily France); 15th through 20th centuries.
100 lighting devices (including betty lamps, candlesticks, grease lamps, rush holders, lanterns); brass, bronze, iron, pewter, tinware (some painted); USA; 18th and 19th centuries.

Metalwork: Base Metals
150 brass boxes, frames, lighting devices, hardware, tablewares; Austria, Belgium, England, France, Germany, India, Italy, Netherlands, Tibet, USA; 17th through 20th centuries.
100 bronze figures, furniture, hardware, matchboxes, medals; Austria, Belgium, Canada, Egypt, England, France, Germany, India, Italy, Persia, Philippines, Spain, Tibet, USA; 1st century B.C. and 15th through 20th centuries.
small collection of copper food molds, frames, lighting devices, plaques; France, Germany, Italy, Mexico, North Africa, Iran, Spain, USA; 16th through 20th centuries.
100 iron architectural fittings, candlesticks, lanterns, locks and keys; England, France, Germany, Italy, Netherlands, Spain, USA; (primarily Spain); 15th through 19th centuries.
100 pewter candlesticks, desk items, tablewares; Austria, Bohemia, France, Germany, Netherlands, USA, (primarily Germany); 18th through 20th centuries.
30 steel objects including furniture, edged weapons, tablewares; Austria, Denmark, England, France, Germany, Italy, Japan, USA; 16th through 20th centuries.
50 tinware examples, some painted, boxes, candlesticks, sconces, tablewares, tewares, vases; England, France, USA; 18th through 19th centuries.
1,500 gilt-bronze and brass furniture mounts; England, France, Germany, Italy, Netherlands, Spain, USA, (primarily France); 15th through 19th centuries.
1,200 *tsuba* and other sword fittings of iron and various alloys; Japan; 12th through 19th centuries.

Metalwork: Precious Metals

1,000 silver boxes, candlesticks, figures, flatware, and tableware items; Austria, Belgium, Bhutan, China, Denmark, England, France, Germany, India, Ireland, Italy, Japan, Mexico, Netherlands, Norway, Sweden, Peru, Poland, Prussia, Russia, Spain, Switzerland, Turkey, USA, Venezuela, (primarily England, France, USA); 15th through 20th centuries.

35 gold personal accessories, buttons, boxes, tablewares, walking sticks; China, England, France, Germany, Italy, Russia, Switzerland, USA; 18th through 20th centuries.

Other Materials

small collection of bone, crystal, horn, jade, shell, tortoiseshell boxes, combs, figures, measuring devices, table screens, seals, snuff bottles, vessels; China, Egypt, England, France, Germany, Italy, Japan, North Africa; 16th through 19th centuries.

40 leather boxes, bookcovers, cases, wall hangings; Austria, Belgium, China, France, Germany, Italy, Japan, North Africa, USA; 16th through 20th centuries.

50 marble candlesticks, clocks, desk items, samples, seals; France, Greece, Italy, Norway, Portugal, Spain, USA (primarily Italy); 18th through 20th centuries.

small collection of paper and papier-mâché objects; boxes, furniture, wall panels; England, France, Italy, USA; 18th and 19th centuries.

small collection of strawwork baskets, boxes, lamps, étuis; Bhutan, France, India; 18th through 20th centuries.

Timepieces and Measuring Devices

40 clocks (including mantel, table, tall, traveling, wall) and watches; gilt bronze, enamel, precious metals, porcelain; England, France, Germany, Japan, Netherlands, Scotland, Sweden, Switzerland, Turkey, USA; 17th through 20th centuries.

small collection of measuring and optical devices; China, England, France, Germany, USA; 18th through 20th centuries.

Toys and Games

125 puppets and 350 theatrical props made and used by Frank and Elizabeth Haines; USA; 1920–50.

30 puppets and marionettes and a marionette theater; England, France, Italy; 18th through 19th centuries.

50 games, puzzles, and toys; Austria, China, England, France, Germany, Italy, Japan, USA; 17th through 20th centuries.

FINDING AIDS

Card catalog arranged by accession number, object type, and material. Supplementary index of makers' names.

Research files are maintained on individual objects, artists, and subjects (e.g., lighting devices, Scandinavian design).

The Department contains a special collection of photographs and related materials pertaining to the furniture of Eugenio Quarti (1867–1931) and Mario Quarti (1901–1974).

SELECTED PUBLICATIONS

Dauterman, Carl. *Buttons in the Collection of the Cooper-Hewitt Museum.* New York: Cooper-Hewitt Museum, 1982.
This booklet traces the history of buttons as reflected in the Cooper-Hewitt Collection. Many illustrations.

McFadden, David Revere. *Furniture in the Collection of the Cooper-Hewitt Museum.* New York: Cooper-Hewitt Museum, 1979.
This booklet contains a historical essay concerning important furniture designers, craftsmen, and manufacturers, as well as wide range of types and styles of furniture. Illustrated are twenty-two American, Oriental, and European examples dating from the 17th through the 20th centuries.

––––––. *Glass in the Collection of the Cooper-Hewitt Museum.* New York: Cooper-Hewitt Museum, 1979.
This historical essay traces glassmaking and ornamentation from the ancient Egyptian period through the present day. Described are production techniques—glass blowing, molding, and pressing—and decoration techniques such as enameling, gilding, cutting, engraving, etching, and chemical coloration. Twenty-five pieces from the Museum's collection are illustrated.

––––––. *Porcelain in the Collection of the Cooper-Hewitt Museum.* New York: Cooper-Hewitt Museum, 1979.
The history of porcelain throughout the world is described in this essay. There are illustrations of twenty examples of American, European, and Oriental porcelain, dating from the 17th through the 20th centuries.

––––––. *Pottery in the Collection of the Cooper-Hewitt Museum.* New York: Cooper-Hewitt Museum, 1981.
This booklet contains a worldwide historical overview of earthenware emphasizing decoration, form, function, and technique. Twenty-two pieces are illustrated.

––––––. *Silver in the Collection of the Cooper-Hewitt Museum.* New York: Cooper-Hewitt Museum, 1980.
The essay in this booklet traces the history of European silver guilds and American silversmithing as well as the development of silver design, forms, and ornamentation. Twenty-eight pieces in the collection are illustrated. Biographical information concerning the craftsmen is included.

––––––. *Tiles in the Collection of the Cooper-Hewitt Museum.* New York: Cooper-Hewitt Museum, 1980.
The history of tilemaking over the past 400 years is described in this essay. American, English, Continental, and Middle Eastern tiles, all from the collection, are illustrated.

Patterson, Jerry E. *Matchsafes in the Collection of the Cooper-Hewitt Museum.* New York: Cooper-Hewitt Museum, 1981.
The essay in this booklet traces the history of friction matches, and the subsequent development of matchsafes—their design, materials, motifs, and

ornamentation. More than 135 examples from the Museum's Brener Collection are illustrated.

Rosin, Dr. Henry. *Tsuba and Japanese Sword Fittings in the Collection of the Cooper-Hewitt Museum*. New York: Cooper-Hewitt Museum, 1980.

This essay briefly surveys the history of Japanese swords as well as the history of major schools of *tsuba* artists. Forty-seven objects are illustrated from the George Cameron Stone Collection.

LENDING POLICY

Loans may be granted to not-for-profit educational institutions for exhibitions. Loans must be approved by the Loan Committee and the Director of the Museum. Inquiries should be addressed to the Curator, Department of Decorative Arts, Cooper-Hewitt Museum.

PHOTODUPLICATION SERVICE

Available at prevailing rates, subject to rules and procedures of the Department and Museum. Inquiries should be addressed to the Curator, Department of Decorative Arts, Cooper-Hewitt Museum.

PUBLIC ACCESS

Exhibition galleries closed Monday, open Tuesday 10 to 9, Wednesday through Saturday 10 to 5, Sunday 12 to 5. Entrance fee. Research inquiries and requests for information concerning objects not currently on view should be addressed to the

Curator, Department of Decorative Arts
Cooper-Hewitt Museum
2 East 91st Street
New York, N.Y. 10028

2_B

Department of Textiles

The Department of Textiles comprehensive and representative collection illustrates the history of textiles, their design, decoration, and trade throughout the world, from the 3rd century B.C. to the present day. Holdings of 20,000 items document the development of structures, processes, and techniques—specifically the history of weaving, needlework, dyeing, and printing. At the same time, these collections record the development of textile styles and patterns, and the history of the cotton, silk, and wool trade among the countries of the Near and Far East, Europe, and the United States.

The Department's encyclopedic embroidery and lace collections encompass costume, domestic, and ecclesiastical forms dating from the 6th through the

20th centuries. While the collection is unique for its sizable holdings of rare early materials (Byzantine, Coptic, Classical Egyptian, Egypto-Arabic, Hispano-Moresque, and Persian), the majority of the embroideries and laces date from the 17th through the 19th centuries.

Yet another comprehensive collection is composed of printed cotton textiles. There are significant holdings of both Indian painted cottons (chintz) dating as early as the 15th century, and the European printed fabrics which were inspired by these earlier Far Eastern imports.

Another important collection of European printed textiles includes 18th- and early 19th-century French printed fabrics and related designers' drawings.

The history of silk fabric production is documented by collections from three geographical and cultural areas. The earliest group of silks, dating from the 8th through 13th centuries, are from the Islamic Mediterranean and Near Eastern areas. Medieval silks from Italy, Sicily, and Spain are complemented by later western European examples which illustrate the development of the silk industry on that continent.

The oldest and perhaps most important objects in the entire Textile Collection are a bonnet and pair of mitts, all of silk. These Chinese items were made during the late Eastern Chou period, about the 3rd century B.C., and were excavated from the site at Ch'ang-sha.

The Department holds several unique collections including a group of spectacular European white linen tassels made during the 16th and 17th centuries. Another rarity is a group of woven and embroidered French silk waistcoats (along with designs and samples) made in the high style of the 18th and early 19th centuries.

Technical processes for textile production are thoroughly documented in holdings of pattern, printing, sample, and swatch books, loom and weaving instructions, and dyer's manuals and recipes. Most of these notebooks and volumes are European and date from the 19th century.

CLASSIFIED CATALOG OF OBJECTS

Textiles

large and comprehensive collection of embroidery in a full range of techniques (including pictures, costume, domestic, and ecclesiastical items); Central Asia, Europe, Near East, Indonesia (primarily Europe); 6th through 20th centuries.

small and representative collection of pre-Columbian and Spanish Colonial fabrics; South America; 8th through 17th centuries.

comprehensive collection of dyed cotton; India; 15th through 19th centuries.

comprehensive collection of lace and lacelike structures including related pattern books (forms include ecclesiastical and costume items; techniques include bobbin lace, crocheting, drawnwork, embroidered net, macrame, netting, knitting, knotting, and tape lace); Europe; 16th through early 19th centuries.

collection of trimmings (including braid, fringe, ribbons, tassels, and other narrow goods); Europe; from the 17th century.

small collection of carpet fragments, carpetbags, and rugs (including cut pile carpet); Europe, USA; 17th and 18th centuries.

comprehensive collection of silk fabrics; Mediterranean and Islamic Mediterranean cultures; 8th through 13th centuries.

woven silk and silk mixture fabrics (including brocades, damasks, and velvets); Europe; 17th through 19th centuries.

tapestries; Low Countries; from the 17th century.

needleworked and woven bedcovers; Europe, USA; 17th through 20th centuries.

large and comprehensive collection of printed fabrics (includes copper plate, roller, screen, wood block printed); Europe; late 17th through 20th centuries.

large collection of printed fabrics and related designers' drawings; France; 18th and early 19th centuries.

380 embroidered coats, suits, waistcoats, related designs, and samples; France; 18th and early 19th centuries.

printed pictures and scarves, some commemorative; China, Europe, USA; 18th through 20th centuries.

embroidered and woven shawls; Middle East; 19th century.

dyers' recipes, pattern, printing, sample, and swatch books, loom and weaving instructions; Europe; 19th century.

small collection of works by fiber artists (including rugs, table linens, wall hangings); England, Scandinavia, USA; 20th century.

resist dyed fabrics (including batik, ikat, stenciled, tie-dyed, and other techniques); India, Indonesia, Japan, USA.

textile printing items (including individual and sets of blocks); England, France, Japan; 19th century.

FINDING AIDS
Card catalog arranged by accession number. Index of designers represented in the collection.

SELECTED PUBLICATIONS
Beer, Alice Baldwin. *Trade Goods: A Study of Indian Chintz in the Collection of the Cooper-Hewitt Museum*. Washington, D.C.: Smithsonian Institution Press, 1970.
> This exhibition catalog traces the history of the trade and techniques of production of Indian painted and dyed chintz. Thirty textile items from the collection are illustrated.

Sonday, Milton. *Lace in the Collection of the Cooper-Hewitt Museum*. New York: Cooper-Hewitt Museum, 1982.
> This booklet traces the history of lace as reflected in the Cooper-Hewitt Collection. Many illustrations.

Sonday, Milton and Gillian Moss.*Western European Embroidery in the Collection of the Cooper-Hewitt Museum*. New York: Cooper-Hewitt Museum, 1978.
> This booklet contains highlights from the embroidery collection. Techniques and the historical development of western European embroidery are discussed. Twenty pieces are illustrated.

LENDING POLICY
Loans may be granted to not-for-profit educational institutions for exhibitions. Loans must be approved by the Loan Committee and the Director of the Museum. Inquiries should be addressed to the Curator, Department of Textiles, Cooper-Hewitt Museum.

PHOTODUPLICATION SERVICE
Available at prevailing rates, subject to rules and procedures of the Department and Museum. Inquiries should be addressed to the Curator, Department of Textiles, Cooper-Hewitt Museum.

PUBLIC ACCESS
Exhibition galleries closed Monday, open Tuesday 10 to 9, Wednesday through Saturday 10 to 5, Sunday 12 to 5. Entrance fee. Research inquiries and requests for information concerning objects not currently on view should be addressed to the

Curator, Department of Textiles
Cooper-Hewitt Museum
2 East 91st Street
New York, N.Y. 10028

2c

Department of Wallpaper

The Department of Wallpaper contains the largest assemblage of wallcoverings in America. Of particular interest to decorative arts and cultural historians are the large holdings of documented and dated papers found in American homes from the 18th century to the present day. Late 18th and early 19th century French and English wallcoverings are particularly numerous and notable, although European examples from the 17th century are also represented. In addition to wallcoverings, there is a related collection of early to mid-19th century paper-covered boxes.

CLASSIFIED CATALOG OF OBJECTS

Wall Coverings and Hangings
6,000 wallpaper samples, fireboards, doors, and window shades; China, England, France, Germany, Italy, Japan, Netherlands, Sweden, Switzerland, USA; 17th through 20th centuries.
70 wall covering fragments; leather; Belgium, Netherlands; 17th and 18th centuries.

80 wallpaper sample books; England, France, Germany, Switzerland, USA; early to mid-20th centuries.

30 wall coverings of imitation leather; England, France, Japan, USA; late 19th through 20th centuries.

40 wallpaper production items (designs, printing blocks, rollers, stencils); France, USA; late 18th through mid-20th centuries.

70 boxes and bandboxes; USA; early to mid-19th century.

FINDING AIDS

Card catalog arranged by accession number, object type, and material.

SELECTED PUBLICATIONS

Lynn, Catherine. *Wallpaper in America: From the Seventeenth Century to World War I.* New York: W. W. Norton & Co., 1980.

This volume is a comprehensive study of wallpaper typically used in America from the 17th century to 1915. Patterns and their usage in specific rooms throughout the house are recorded. More than 175 papers from the Cooper-Hewitt's collection are illustrated.

———. *Wallpaper in the Collection of the Cooper-Hewitt Museum.* New York: Cooper-Hewitt Museum, 1981.

This booklet traces the history of wallpaper design, production, and use in Europe and America from the 17th through the 20th centuries. Samples in the collection are illustrated.

LENDING POLICY

Loans may be granted to not-for-profit educational institutions for exhibitions. Loans must be approved by the Loan Committee and the Director of the Museum. Inquiries should be addressed to the Curator, Department of Wallpaper, Cooper-Hewitt Museum.

PHOTODUPLICATION SERVICE

Available at prevailing rates, subject to rules and procedures of the Department and Museum. Inquiries should be addressed to the Curator, Department of Wallpaper, Cooper-Hewitt Museum.

PUBLIC ACCESS

Exhibition galleries closed Monday, open Tuesday 10 to 9, Wednesday through Saturday 10 to 5, Sunday 12 to 5. Entrance fee. Research inquiries and requests for information concerning objects not currently on view should be addressed to the

Curator, Department of Wallpaper
Cooper-Hewitt Museum
2 East 91st Street
New York, N.Y. 10028

3

Freer Gallery of Art

In 1906 Charles Lang Freer gave his collection of American and Oriental art to the Smithsonian Institution with the stated purpose that it be used to further the study of civilizations of the Far East and to promote the highest ideals of beauty. The Freer Gallery's original objectives have been expanded to include the study of Near Eastern civilizations.

The Freer Gallery of Art, designed by Charles A. Platt and completed in 1921, houses one of the world's finest collections of Chinese, Japanese, Korean, and Near Eastern art. Among its holdings of approximately 12,000 works of art are important Chinese bronzes, ceramics, lacquer, stone sculpture, and archaic

7   Ashiya-type kettle, Namboku-chō period, 1333–1392 A.D.
Japan.
Iron.

jades; Japanese ceramics and lacquerware; Korean ceramics; and Near Eastern ceramics, glass, and metalwork.

Within the Museum is a Study Collection comprising approximately 5,000 pottery shards and bronze fragments, of all periods and a wide variety of origins, as well as small collections of lacquerware, cloisonné enamel, wall paintings, and other forms. These materials are not used for exhibition but are available for comparison, laboratory analysis, and other educational purposes.

FINDING AIDS

Card catalog arranged by accession number.

Complete card index by broad subject heading (e.g., bronze, glass, pottery, etc.) arranged by place and date of origin.

SELECTED PUBLICATIONS

Ettinghausen, Richard. *Ancient Glass in the Freer Gallery of Art.* Washington, D.C.: Freer Gallery of Art, 1962.

This exhibition catalog illustrates Egyptian, Roman, Christian, Islamic, and

8 *Peacock Room,* south wall and sideboard, 1876–77.
By James McNeill Whistler, USA.
Oil color and gold on leather and wood.

9 Disc (*pi*), Eastern Han dynasty, A.D. 25–220.
China.
Jade.

Chinese glass from the collection.

Freer Gallery of Art. *Arts of Asia at the Time of American Independence*. Washington, D.C.: Freer Gallery of Art, 1976.

This exhibition catalog includes screens, furniture, porcelain, and lacquer from the Freer collection, all of which date from the late 18th century.

Freer Gallery of Art. *The Freer Gallery of Art, I China. The Freer Gallery of Art, II Japan*. Both published Tokyo, Japan: Kodansha, 1971. Reprinted 1981.

Using a selection of Chinese and Japanese objects from the collection, these volumes include bronze, enamel, gold, jade, porcelain, and silver. Explanatory text notes iconographic details and historical and stylistic changes.

Freer Gallery of Art. *Masterpieces of Chinese and Japanese Art: Freer Gallery of Art Handbook*. Washington, D.C.: Freer Gallery of Art, 1976.

This volume illustrates 243 of the most outstanding examples of Chinese and Japanese art at the Freer Gallery. Basic information about the Gallery is also included.

Hobbs, Susan. *The Whistler Peacock Room*. Washington, D.C.: Freer Gallery of Art, 1980.

This booklet describes, illustrates, and traces the history of the Peacock Room which is exhibited in the Gallery.

Murray, Julia K. *A Decade of Discovery: Selected Acquisitions 1970–1980*. Washington, D.C.: Freer Gallery of Art, 1979.

This catalog publishes the most outstanding of the objects that entered the collection of the Freer Gallery during the 1970s. A great range of artifacts from China, Japan, Korea, India, Southeast Asia, Iran, Turkey, and Syria are presented. The types of media represented in the exhibition include pottery, painting, sculpture, metalwork, lacquerware, and jade.

Pope, John A.; Knapp, Josephine H.; and Atil, Esin. *Oriental Ceramics: The World's Great Collections, The Freer Gallery of Art*. Tokyo, Japan: Kodansha, 1975. Reprinted 1981.
This volume describes and illustrates 420 ceramic pieces from the collection.

Ars Orientalis. Issued jointly by the Freer Gallery of Art and the Fine Arts Department, University of Michigan. 1–. 1954–.
Occasional Papers. Washington, D.C.: Freer Gallery of Art, 1–. 1947–.
Oriental Studies. Washington, D.C.: Freer Gallery of Art, 1–. 1933–.
These three irregularly published papers are devoted to the subject areas in which the Freer Gallery specializes, and often contain articles on objects in the Freer collection.

A continuing series of leaflets distributed free in the galleries is in production. Currently leaflets are available on the following topics (and others not directly pertinent to this survey): Chinese Bronzes, Chinese Sculpture, Islamic Ceramics, Japanese Screens, Japanese Ceramics, and Ancient Chinese Jade.

LENDING POLICY
The terms of the Freer bequest prohibit the loan of objects given by Charles Lang Freer. Selected objects in the Study Collection may be lent, subject to rules and procedures of the Gallery.

PUBLIC ACCESS
Exhibition galleries open to the public from 10–5:30 daily except Christmas. Research inquiries and information concerning objects not on exhibition should be addressed to the

Director
Freer Gallery of Art
Smithsonian Institution
Washington, D.C. 20560

3A

American Art Collection

The Freer Gallery of Art houses one of the world's two largest collections of works by James A. McNeill Whistler including the famous "Peacock Room," the only surviving example of Whistler's artistry applied to an architectural interior.

There is also a collection of Pewabic pottery made by Mary Chase Perry (Stratton) of Detroit. Freer's collection of early Chinese pottery inspired Perry to use overglaze decoration in her work.

CLASSIFIED CATALOG OF OBJECTS

Ceramics
35 earthenware pieces of Pewabic pottery; Detroit; 1903–16.

Furniture
small collection of furniture made for Charles Lang Freer's home (including several chairs by the A. H. Davenport Co.); Boston; ca. 1892–1911.

FINDING AIDS
Card catalog arranged by accession number.
Complete card index by broad subject heading (e.g., bronze, glass, pottery, etc.) arranged by place and date of origin.

LENDING POLICY
The terms of the Freer bequest prohibit the loan of objects given by Charles Lang Freer. Selected objects in the Study Collection may be lent, subject to rules and procedures of the Gallery.

PUBLIC ACCESS
Exhibition galleries open to the public from 10–5:30 daily except Christmas. Research inquiries and information concerning objects not on exhibition should be addressed to the

Curator, American Art Collection
Freer Gallery of Art
Smithsonian Institution
Washington, D.C. 20560

3B

Chinese Art Collection

The Freer Gallery of Art has important and comprehensive collections of Chinese bronzes, ceramics, and archaic jades, totaling 2,500 objects, dating from the Neolithic period through the Ch'ing dynasties. The bronzes from the Shang, Chou, and Han dynasties, mainly ritual vessels, are of rare quality and breadth. The history of Chinese ceramics from the Neolithic period through the Ch'ing dynasty is documented in the Freer collection. Holdings include several unique pieces from the Neolithic period, Shang, Han, and T'ang dynasties. From the Sung dynasty, monochrome-glazed ware, celadons, Tz'u-chou ware, white wares, and porcelains are well represented. Holdings from later dynasties (Yüan, Ming, Ch'ing) include comprehensive groups of blue-and-white porcelain, I-hsing ware, monochrome-glazed ware, and enameled ware.

The important jade collection contains ceremonial implements and weapons dating from the Neolithic period through the Ch'ing dynasty. Artifacts from the early periods are most numerous and significant.

CLASSIFIED CATALOG OF OBJECTS

Ceramics

500 earthenware, stoneware, and porcelain figures, tomb models, vessels; China; Neolithic period through Ch'ing dynasties.

Furniture

small collection of furniture (primarily chairs and tables); China; Ming and Ch'ing dynasties.

Glass

small collection of glass dishes, figures, and rings; China; late Chou through Ch'ing dynasties.

Lacquer

40 lacquer boxes, dishes, musical instruments, ornaments, panels; China; Eastern Chou, Ming, Sung, Yüan, and Ch'ing dynasties.

Metalwork: Base Metals

1,000 bronze bells, belt hooks, chariot fittings, figures, jewelry, masks, mirrors, ornaments, ritual vessels, weapons; China; Shang through Ming dynasties.

30 iron and lead figures, garment clasps, mirrors, musical instruments; China; Chou, Ming, and Ch'ing dynasties.

Metalwork: Precious Metals

30 gold and silver hair ornaments, vessels, and jewelry; China; Chou through Ch'ing dynasties.

Other Materials

800 jade ceremonial implements, ornaments, sculptural forms, vessels; China; Neolithic period through Ch'ing dynasties.

200 stone relief carvings and sculptural forms; China; Shang through Ch'ing dynasties.

small collection of carved wood figures, ornaments, seals, and other carvings; China; Ming and Ch'ing dynasties.

Textiles

180 silk mats, panels, tapestries, wall hangings; China; T'ang, Yüan, Ming, and Ch'ing dynasties.

FINDING AIDS

Card catalog arranged by accession number.

Complete card index by broad subject heading (e.g., bronze, glass, pottery, etc.) arranged by place and date of origin.

SELECTED PUBLICATIONS

Freer Gallery of Art. *Ming Porcelains in the Freer Gallery of Art*. Washington, D.C.: Freer Gallery of Art, 1953.

This booklet illustrates and briefly describes approximately thirty pieces in the collection.

Pope, John A.; Gettens, Rutherford J.; Cahill, James; and Barnard, Noel. *The Freer Chinese Bronzes, Volume I*. Washington, D.C.: Freer Gallery of Art, 1967.

Gettens, Rutherford J. *The Freer Chinese Bronzes, Volume II*. Washington, D.C.: Freer Gallery of Art, 1969.

These two volumes describe 122 Chinese ritual bronzes in the collection. Complete catalog and technical information is included.

LENDING POLICY

The terms of the Freer bequest prohibit the loan of objects given by Charles Lang Freer. Selected objects in the Study Collection may be lent, subject to rules and procedures of the Gallery.

PUBLIC ACCESS

Exhibition galleries open to the public from 10–5:30 daily except Christmas. Research inquiries and information concerning objects not on exhibition should be addressed to the

Curator, Chinese Art Collection
Freer Gallery of Art
Smithsonian Institution
Washington, D.C. 20560

3c

Japanese Art Collection

The Freer Gallery of Art is well known for its collection of Japanese ceramics from the Jōmon through Meiji periods. Numerous artists, potters, types, sites, and wares are included in this group which reflects many aspects of the history of Japanese ceramics.

Holdings of exceptional lacquered boxes, *inrō*, furniture, and sculpture date primarily from the Muromachi through Meiji periods.

CLASSIFIED CATALOG OF OBJECTS

Architectural Elements

150 folding screens and sliding door panels; Japan; Muromachi through Meiji periods.

Ceramics
800 earthenware, stoneware, and porcelain wares; Japan; Jōmon through Meiji periods.

Costume (Garments and Accessories)
100 embroidered and brocaded robes and sashes; Japan; Edo and Meiji periods.

Lacquer
75 lacquer boxes, inrō, netsuke, relief sculpture, and pieces of furniture; Japan; Nara through Meiji periods.

Metalwork: Base Metals
50 bronze and iron bells, figures, mirrors, ritual ornaments and implements, and vessels; Japan; primarily Kamakura and Meiji periods.

Other Materials
45 wooden masks, netsuke, panels, and sculptures; Japan; Suiko through Edo periods.

FINDING AIDS
Card catalog arranged by accession number.
Complete card index by broad subject heading (e.g., bronze, glass, pottery, etc.) arranged by place and date of origin.

SELECTED PUBLICATIONS
Yonemura, Ann. *Japanese Lacquer*. Washington, D.C.: Freer Gallery of Art, 1979. This exhibition catalog illustrates fifty-seven selected examples from the Freer Gallery collection. Containers, furniture, sculpture, and ceramic repairs are discussed.

LENDING POLICY
The terms of the Freer bequest prohibit the loan of objects given by Charles Lang Freer. Selected objects in the Study Collection may be lent, subject to rules and procedures of the Gallery.

PUBLIC ACCESS
Exhibition galleries open to the public from 10–5:30 daily except Christmas. Research inquiries and information concerning objects not on exhibition should be addressed to the

Curator, Japanese Art Collection
Freer Gallery of Art
Smithsonian Institution
Washington, D.C. 20560

3D

Korean Art Collection

The Korean Art Collection is composed primarily of ceramic objects ranging from the Silla through the Yi periods. From the Koryŏ period, there is an outstanding collection of celadon vessels, while from the later Yi period Punch'ong ware, other stoneware, and porcelain are well represented.

CLASSIFIED CATALOG OF OBJECTS

Ceramics
350 stoneware and porcelain boxes and vessels; Korea; Three Kingdoms through Yi dynasties.

Metalwork: Base Metals
150 bronze ornaments, spoons, and vessels; Korea; Three Kingdoms and Koryŏ dynasties.

Metalwork: Precious Metals
small collection of gold earrings and ornaments; Korea; Silla period.
small collection of silver spoons; Korea; Koryŏ dynasty.

FINDING AIDS
Card catalog arranged by accession number.
Complete card index by broad subject heading (e.g., bronze, glass, pottery, etc.) arranged by place and date of origin.

LENDING POLICY
The terms of the Freer bequest prohibit the loan of objects given by Charles Lang Freer. Selected objects in the Study Collection may be lent, subject to rules and procedures of the Gallery.

PUBLIC ACCESS
Exhibition galleries open to the public from 10–5:30 daily except Christmas. Research inquiries and information concerning objects not on exhibition should be addressed to the

Curator, Korean Art Collection
Freer Gallery of Art
Smithsonian Institution
Washington, D.C. 20560

3E

Near Eastern Art Collection

This 1,700 object collection documents the development of pottery, glass, and metalwork in Egypt, Syria, Iraq, Iran, Turkey, Afghanistan, Pakistan, and India during the pre-Islamic, Islamic, and Christian periods. There are exceptional holdings of ancient Egyptian and Syrian glass as well as Islamic glass, metalwork, and pottery. The Freer Gallery's unparalleled collection of 1,000 Buddhist, Christian, Hindu, and Islamic manuscripts, including bound volumes and single folios, dates from the 3rd through the 19th centuries. These manuscripts are described in detail in the *Finders' Guide to Prints and Drawings in the Smithsonian Institution* by Lynda C. Claassen.

CLASSIFIED CATALOG OF OBJECTS

Ceramics

600 earthenware fragments, ornaments, plaques, tiles, vessels; Egypt, Iran, Iraq, Syria, Turkey; 15th century B.C. through 19th century A.D.

Glass

1,300 glass amulets, beads, inlay fragments, plaques, vessels; Egypt, Europe, Iran, Syria; 15th century B.C. to 14th century A.D.

Metalwork: Base Metals

small collection of brass and bronze figures and vessels; Egypt, India, Iran, Syria, Turkey; 4th century B.C. through 17th century A.D.

Metalwork: Precious Metals

small collection of gold and silver jewelry and vessels, some with enamel decoration; Egypt, Iran, Syria; 5th century B.C. to 17th century A.D.

Other Materials

jade jug; Turkey; 16th century A.D.
wood shrine with figure; Egypt; 4th century B.C.
rock crystal flask; Egypt; 9th to 10th centuries.
35 stone religious figures and sculptures; Egypt, India, Iran, eastern Mediterranean area; 24th century B.C. to 12th century A.D.

Textiles

small collection of brocades and velvets; India, Iran, Turkey; 16th through 18th centuries A.D.

FINDING AIDS

Card catalog arranged by accession number.
Complete card index by broad subject heading (e.g., bronze, glass, pottery, etc.) arranged by place and date of origin.

SELECTED PUBLICATIONS

Atil, Esin. *Art of the Arab World*. Washington, D.C.: Freer Gallery of Art, 1975.
This exhibition catalog includes 80 objects from the Freer collection. Metal-work, pottery, and crystal from Egypt, Iraq, and Syria made between the 8th and 16th centuries are illustrated.

————. *Ceramics from the World of Islam*. Washington, D.C.: Freer Gallery of Art, 1973.
Diverse techniques, styles, and regional developments are represented in these 101 pieces of pottery from the collection.

————. *Exhibition of 2500 Years of Persian Art*. Washington, D.C.: Freer Gallery of Art, 1981.
Architectural details, ceramics, and metalwork of diverse provenances, types, and techniques are included in this exhibition catalog of the Freer collection.

————. *Turkish Art of the Ottoman Period*. Washington, D.C.: Freer Gallery of Art, 1973.
The jade, pottery, and tiles included in this exhibition catalog represent the early and classical periods of Ottoman art.

Ettinghausen, Richard. *Medieval Near Eastern Ceramics in the Freer Gallery of Art*. Baltimore, Maryland: Lord Baltimore Press, 1960.
This booklet discusses ceramic art of the Islamic world and illustrates thirty-four important pieces in the collection.

LENDING POLICY

The terms of the Freer bequest prohibit the loan of objects given by Charles Lang Freer. Selected objects in the Study Collection may be lent, subject to rules and procedures of the Gallery.

PUBLIC ACCESS

Exhibition galleries open to the public from 10–5:30 daily except Christmas. Re-search inquiries and information concerning objects not on exhibition should be addressed to the

Curator, Near Eastern Art Collection
Freer Gallery of Art
Smithsonian Institution
Washington, D.C. 20560

4

Hirshhorn Museum and Sculpture Garden

The Hirshhorn Museum and Sculpture Garden is the permanent home of the distinguished collection of contemporary painting and sculpture given to the United States by Connecticut financier Joseph H. Hirshhorn. In 1966, the Congress provided the site and authorized funding for construction of the Museum which opened to the public in October 1974. The complex comprises an outdoor sunken sculpture garden, plaza areas for sculpture surrounding the Museum

10 Two windows from the Martin House,
    Buffalo, New York, 1904.
    Designed by Frank Lloyd Wright.
    USA.
    Stained glass with lead.

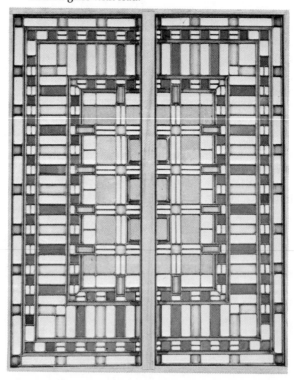

11 Chess set, 1953.
    Designed and made by Max Ernst.
    France.
    Wood.

and the Museum proper, and an unusual circular building with a huge bronze fountain dominating its inner plaza designed by Gordon Bunshaft of Skidmore, Owings, and Merrill.

In Mr. Hirshhorn's original gift were more than 2,000 sculptures and 4,000 paintings including the works of such masters as Eakins, Homer, Rodin, Moore, Matisse, and de Kooning. Also part of the gift were some sixty objects of particular interest to students of the decorative arts and another 219 objects of related interest. Among the former are modern stained-glass windows, pre-Columbian ceramic vessels, and ancient ceramic, glass, and bronze objects. Works of related interest include Benin bronzes, pre-Columbian ceramic figures, South Arabian alabaster sculptures, and Egyptian funerary art.

CLASSIFIED CATALOG OF OBJECTS

Architectural Elements

6 stained-glass windows designed by Frank Lloyd Wright; from the Coonley
   Playhouse, Chicago, Illinois, and the Martin House, Buffalo, New York; 1912
   and 1904, respectively.

Ceramics

8 terra-cotta vessels; Amlash, Chorasan, and Minai cultures, Iran; 1300 to 1000
   B.C.
1 terra-cotta pitcher *oinochoe*; Etruscan; 600 to 500 B.C.

12 Jug, eighteenth century.
Benin culture, Africa.
Bronze.

5 terra-cotta figures; Mediterranean area and Near East, including Sumerian,
Etruscan, and Greek cultures; 25th to 1st centuries B.C.

2 terra-cotta heads, one figure; Benin culture, Africa; 16th to 18th centuries.

82 terra-cotta figures; pre-Columbian cultures, Middle America; 15 century B.C.
to 15th century A.D.

20 earthenware vessels; Chupicuaro, Colima, Michoacan, Mixtec, Nayarit, Tla-
tilco, Vera Cruz, Zapotec pre-Columbian cultures, Mexico; 15th century B.C.
to 15th century A.D.

Glass

2 glass vessels; Eastern Mediterranean; Syrio-Roman and Islamic periods.

Metalwork: Base Metals

2 bronze horse bits; Etruscan; 800 to 700 B.C.

1 bronze jug; Benin culture, Africa; 18th century.

4 bronze goldweights; Ashanti culture, Africa; 19th to 20th centuries.

1 bronze jug; Benin culture, Africa; 19th to 20th centuries.

1 iron figure of a horse; USA; early 19th century.

2 bronze and 1 plaster cast for the *Mirror of Venus* by A. B. Davies; USA; early
20th century.

1 bronze doorknocker and 2 bronze garden ornaments by Henri Gaudier-Brzeska
and G. Lachaise; Great Britain and USA; early 20th century.

25 bronze figures; Mediterranean and Near East including Egyptian, Etruscan,

Greek, Hittite, Iberian, Iranian, Sardinian, Sumerian cultures; 21st century to 1st century B.C.

33 bronze figures, plaques, heads and ceremonial objects; Benin culture, Africa; 16th to 20th centuries.

3 iron figures; Bambara and Senufo cultures, Africa; 19th to 20th centuries.

Metalwork: Precious Metals

3 gold pendants; Baule culture, Africa; 20th century.

1 gold pectoral fragment; Ziwiye, Iran; 800 to 700 B.C.

Other Materials

22 figures of stone, lava, jade; pre-Columbian cultures, Middle America; 7th century B.C. to 15th century A.D.

8 wood figures, 1 mask; West and Central Africa; 20th century.

16 polychrome wooden mummy masks; Egypt; 2nd century.

18 figures, heads, and reliefs of carved basalt, marble, alabaster, limestone, calcite; Egyptian, Greek, South Arabian, Sumerian, and Anatolian cultures; 3000 B.C. to 2nd century A.D.

2 alabaster and onyx jars; pre-Columbian cultures, Mexico; 4th century B.C. to 15th century A.D.

one wood cigar store figure *Columbia*; USA; 19th century.

Toys and Games

2 wood dolls *akua ba*; Ashanti culture, Africa; early 20th century.

3 chess sets, 1 each by Max Ernst, Man Ray, Larry Rivers; USA; 1953, 1962, and 1959–60, respectively.

FINDING AIDS

Computer printout available for entire collection. Information includes title, artist, medium, date of work, and origin.

LENDING POLICY

Objects are lent to institutions for exhibition. Borrowing institutions must file a facilities report concerning the area in which the work is to be exhibited. Loans must be approved by the Conservator, the Chief Curator, and the Director.

PHOTODUPLICATION SERVICE

Available at prevailing rates, subject to rules and procedures of the Hirshhorn Museum and Sculpture Garden.

PUBLIC ACCESS

Galleries open to the public from 10–5:30 daily except Christmas. Research inquiries and information concerning objects not on exhibition should be addressed to

Chief Curator
Hirshhorn Museum and Sculpture Garden
Smithsonian Institution
Washington, D.C. 20560

5

National Museum of African Art

Founded in 1964 the Museum of African Art joined the Smithsonian Institution in 1979. Now named the National Museum of African Art, it currently occupies ten Capitol Hill buildings including Frederick Douglass' first Washington residence.

The Museum collection is used as an educational tool to illustrate the richness of African culture and its unique contributions to American material cul-

13   Window frame.
     Timbuktu, Mali

14 Drum.
Ashanti, Ghana.
Wood, skin.

ture. Holdings of some 9,000 objects include sculpture, musical instruments, metalwork, and textiles from all African nations, with particular emphasis on the cultures of West and Central Africa. The collection also contains the bequest of Eliot Elisofon, renowned *Life* magazine photographer. Elisofon's gift includes his archives of 100,000 negatives, slides, prints, and films taken on assignments in Africa, and more than 725 African artifacts.

CLASSIFIED CATALOG OF OBJECTS

Architectural Elements
wooden elements (including door frames, granary doors, locks, windows); Central and West Africa; early 20th century.

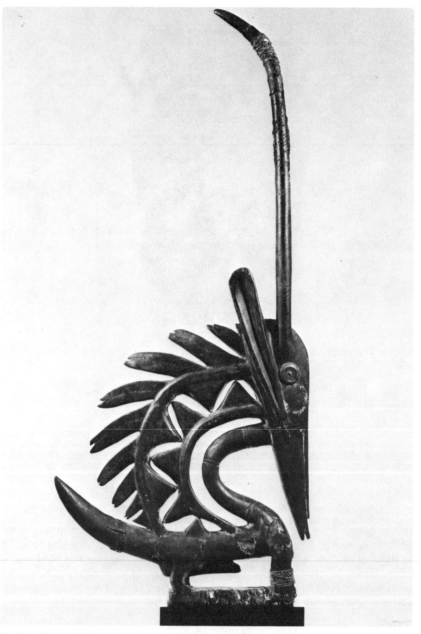

15 Headdress, (chi-wara).
Bambara, Mali.
Wood, metal, rope.

Basketry
45 baskets, containers with lids, fishing traps, fowl carriers, hats, mats, sieves, winnowers; Central and West Africa; early 20th century to present.
125 baskets; Botswana; early 20th century to present.

Ceramics
small collection of earthenware figures, heads, cooking and storage pots, ceremonial vessels; Ethiopia and West Africa; early 20th century to present.

Costume (Garments and Accessories)
small collection of men's cotton robes; Nigeria; mid-20th century.
small collection of men's cotton hats; West Africa, primarily Cameroon and Nigeria; mid-20th century.
small collection of dancers' costumes; Mali, Nigeria, Zaire; early 20th century to present.

Floor Coverings
small collection of grass and textile floor coverings; West Africa and Morocco; early 20th century to present.

Furniture
wooden bed, chairs, headrests, stools (including ceremonial and domestic pieces); West Africa; early 20th century to present.

Metalwork: Base Metals
brass objects (including fans, figures, hand crosses, jewelry, staffs, vessels); Ethiopia, Ghana, Ivory Coast, Mali, Upper Volta; early 20th century to present.
iron objects (including crosses, monies, oil lamps, staffs); Ethiopia, Liberia, Nigeria, Upper Volta; early 20th century to present.
objects (including crosses, jewelry, incense burners) made of various metals and alloys including copper, silver, tin; Ethiopia, North Africa; early 20th century to present.

Musical Instruments
percussion, string, and wind instruments (including bylaphones, drums, harps, horns, rattles, trumpets, whistles, zithers); Central and West Africa; early 20th century to present.

Other Materials
ivory objects (including figures, jewelry, spoons, trumpets, tusks); Central and West Africa; early 20th century to present.
large collection of wood sculpture (including boxes, dolls, figures, game boards, masks, spoons, staffs, vessels); West and Central Africa; early 20th century to present.

Textiles
55 Kuba cloths (a raffia pile cloth); Zaire; early 20th century to present.
475 textile items (including blankets, costume items, tent siding); primarily West Africa; mid-20th century to present.

FINDING AIDS

Card catalogs arranged by accession number and country. Textile collection indexed by country.

SELECTED PUBLICATIONS

Hommel, William L. *African Sculpture: An Exhibition at Princeton University from The Museum of African Art*. Washington, D.C.: Museum of African Art, 1971.
This catalog illustrates 151 wooden sculptural objects from Central and West Africa. All are in the Museum's collection.

Life . . . Afterlife: African Funerary Sculpture. Washington, D.C.: National Museum of African Art, 1981.
This catalog illustrates twelve objects and photographs from the Museum's collection. An essay describes traditional African funerary rituals.

Robbins, Warren. *The Language of African Art: A Guest Exhibition of the Museum of African Art at the Smithsonian Institution*. Washington, D.C.: Museum of African Art, 1970.
This exhibition catalog illustrates thirteen pieces from the Museum's collection.

————. *Tribute to Africa: The Photography and the Collection of Eliot Elisofon: A Memorial Exhibition at the Museum of African Art*. Washington, D.C.: Museum of African Art, 1974.
This catalog includes illustrations of twenty-nine objects from Elisofon's archives which are now in the Museum's collection, a brief biography, tribute, and his essay entitled "On African Sculpture and Modern Art."

LENDING POLICY

Loans are granted to other museums and to educational institutions. Loans must be approved by the Curator of Collections and are subject to review by the Collections Committee of the National Museum of African Art. Information is available from the Office of the Registrar.

PHOTODUPLICATION SERVICE

Available at prevailing rates, subject to rules and procedures of the Museum. Inquiries should be addressed to National Museum of African Art, Eliot Elisofon Archives.

PUBLIC ACCESS

Exhibition galleries open from 11 to 5 daily except Christmas, noon to 5 weekends. Museum hours may be extended between Memorial Day and Labor Day. Research inquiries and information concerning objects not currently on exhibition should be addressed to

Curator of Collections
National Museum of African Art
Smithsonian Institution
Washington, D.C. 20560

6

National Air and Space Museum

The National Air Museum was established in 1946, and in 1966 Congress authorized the expansion of the collection to include space-related materials. Aviation exhibits were formerly housed both in the Arts and Industries Building and in a World War I temporary structure that was adjacent to the Smithsonian Institution Building. In 1976 the National Air and Space Museum, designed by Gyo Obata, was completed and opened to the public.

16

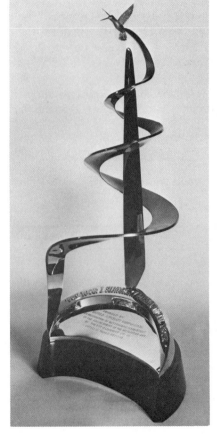

17

16 Igor I. Sikorsky International Flying Trophy, 1961.
Gold, silver, mahogany base.

17 Curtiss Marine Flying Trophy, 1915.
Made by Theodore B. Starr, Inc., New York.
Silver.

The Museum's remarkable collections, which include vehicles and instruments of technological and historical importance, document the development of American aviation and space technology. Among the decorative arts holdings are World War I and II flight materiel (such as uniforms and insignia); examples of 18th and 19th century French ballooning memorabilia; furnishings from the set of the 1975 motion picture *Hindenburg*; tablewares from *Air Force One*; paper kites, including some made for the 1876 Centennial Exposition; and presentation pieces of all varieties.

CLASSIFIED CATALOG OF OBJECTS

Bibelots and Miniatures

small collection of boxes and plaques decorated with ballooning motifs; enamel, ivory, leather, mother-of-pearl, wood; France; 18th and 19th centuries.

medals commemorating U. S. Space flights; USA; 20th century.

religious medals carried by Astronaut Edward H. White II on the *Gemini-4* flight; 20th century.

Ceramics

small collection of tablewares and tiles decorated with ballooning motifs (including Angoulême, Chantilly, Sèvres, Strasbourg); earthenware, stoneware, porcelain; France; 18th and 19th centuries.

small collection of porcelain tablewares; Germany, Japan, USA; 20th century.

Costume (Garments and Accessories)

several thousand articles of flight materiel (primarily military uniforms, medals, insignia, memorabilia); Australia, Europe, Japan, USA; late 18th through 20th centuries.

75 commercial airline uniforms; USA; 20th century.

small collection of fans decorated with ballooning motifs; France; 18th and 19th centuries.

space suits, helmets, and intravehicular coveralls worn by American astronauts; USA; 20th century.

Furniture

small collection of furniture decorated with ballooning motifs; France; 18th and 19th centuries.

Glass

small collection of glass lamps and vessels decorated with ballooning motifs; France; 18th and 19th centuries.

Machinery and Tools

handtool sets from *Apollo* and *Skylab* flights; USA; 20th century.

Metalwork: Base Metals

aluminium *Skylab* tray designed by Raymond Loewy; USA; 1973.

Timepieces and Measuring Devices

small collection of clocks decorated with ballooning motifs; gilt bronze; France; 18th century.

18 Side chair, eighteenth century.
France.
Walnut.

FINDING AIDS
Computerized catalog of the collection.
Supplemental index of the collection arranged by broad subject heading.

SELECTED PUBLICATIONS
Pineau, Roger. *Ballooning: 1782–1972.* Washington, D.C.: Smithsonian Institution Press, 1972.
This exhibition catalog describes the collection's ballooning memorabilia. Several illustrations.

LENDING POLICY
Loans are initiated by the curatorial departments. All loans are subject to the approval by the Director, National Air and Space Museum.

PHOTODUPLICATION SERVICE
Inquiries regarding photographs of objects in the Museum Collection should be addressed to the National Air and Space Museum Library, Photographic Files. Photographs may be ordered at prevailing rates, subject to rules and procedures of the Office of Photographic Services located in the National Museum of American History.

PUBLIC ACCESS
Exhibition galleries open from 10 to 5:30 daily except Christmas. Museum hours may be extended between Memorial Day and Labor Day. Research inquiries and information concerning objects not currently on exhibition should be addressed to the

Registrar
National Air and Space Museum
Smithsonian Institution
Washington, D.C. 20560

7

National Museum of American Art

The National Museum of American Art, formerly the National Collection of Fine Arts, is concerned with American painting, sculpture, and graphic arts from the 18th century to the present. Although formally established in 1906, only since 1968 has the Museum been located in the Patent Office Building, which it shares with the National Portrait Gallery. Two of the Museum's curatorial departments,

19 Necklace, ca. 1895.
    Designed and made by Mellerio Dits
    Meller, Paris.
    Diamonds, enamel, gold.

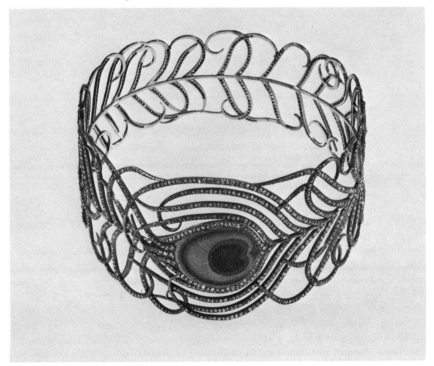

20 Tea urn, late eighteenth century.
South Staffordshire, England.
Enameled brass, brass, ivory.

Renwick Gallery and Alice Pike Barney Studio House, are separately located, exclusively in their own buildings.

The Museum's holdings represent a comprehensive range of American art, with particular strength in the 19th and 20th centuries. Holdings of approximately 2,500 decorative arts objects are primarily the result of John Gellatly's gift in 1929. Notable groups in the Gellatly collection include ancient Egyptian and Syrian glass, English enameled objects, ancient metalwork, and an exceptional collection of European Renaissance jewelry and dress ornaments.

Descriptions follow for the Barney Studio House and Renwick Gallery. All collections, including those used as furnishings in the Barney Studio House and those collected by the Renwick Gallery, are administered and maintained by the National Museum of American Art. They are therefore described as one collection.

7A

Alice Pike Barney Studio House

Alice Pike Barney (1857–1931), an American artist who studied in Paris, built Studio House as a cultural center with a salon atmosphere for Washington's artists and patrons of the arts. It was designed by Waddy Butler Wood in 1904 and renovated in 1979 to reflect the original mood and intent.

During the 1960s, Laura and Natalie Barney, Alice Pike Barney's daughters, donated Studio House to the National Museum of American Art. Additionally, the Barney sisters gave the Museum approximately 800 pieces of American and European furniture, glass, jewelry, and decorative arts to be used as furnishings in the Studio House. They also gave pastels and oils by their mother and her associates as well as photographs of the Barney family and friends. The Barney's small yet superb collections of late 19th century French jewelry and early 20th century French and American glass and bronze lighting devices are particularly notable. Also of interest are a pair of arm chairs designed by Alice Pike Barney and made in Washington's Barney Neighborhood House about 1907.

21 Pendant, ca. 1550–1600.
    Italy.
    Diamonds, enamel, gold, baroque
    pearls, rubies.

7B

Renwick Gallery

The Renwick Gallery was named in honor of its architect, James Renwick, Jr., when it became a part of the Smithsonian Institution in 1965. The building was designed in 1859 to house William Wilson Corcoran's private art collection. As the Corcoran Gallery of Art, it was one of the first structures built specifically as an art gallery in the United States. Today, the Grand Salon is permanently furnished with French parlor furniture, ornamental Sèvres and European enamels which reflect the taste of late 19th century art collectors.

The mission of the Renwick Gallery is to show changing exhibitions emphasizing the creative achievements of American craftsmen and designers. Also, two of the galleries are devoted to temporary exhibitions of art from other countries, often presented under the patronage of the nation concerned.

In 1980 the Renwick Gallery began collecting works by American artists in the craft media—ceramics, fiber, glass, metal, and wood—for its parent Museum, the National Museum of American Art. Holdings now include a small number of examples by artists with distinguished careers in their medium, such

22   Bowls, ca. 1933–53.
     Made by James Prestini, USA.
     Various woods.

as Wendell Castle, Jack Earl, June Schwarcz, Marguerite Wildenhain. Industrial designers who are represented in the collection include Raymond Loewy, Michael Lax, and Peter Schlumbohm.

$7c$

The Collection

CLASSIFIED CATALOG OF OBJECTS

Architectural Elements
small collection of interior and exterior elements; Europe, USA; 11th through 19th centuries.
prizewinning architectural model of proposed Smithsonian Gallery by Eero and Eliel Saarinen; USA; 1939.
pair of bronze-plated cast iron baluster panels designed by George Grant Elmslie for Louis Sullivan for the Carson, Pirie, Scott Building; Chicago; 1899.
iron and brass gates made for the Renwick Gallery by Albert Paley; USA; 1975.

Ceramics
400 porcelain tablewares (including Limoges, le Rosey, Wedgwood); China, England, France; late 19th century.
80 earthenware and porcelain tablewares and vessels; China, Europe, Syria, USA; 6th through 20th centuries.
40 works by contemporary porcelain artists from the juried exhibition *American Porcelain: New Expressions in an Ancient Art* (including Philip Cornelius, Jack Earl, Frank Fleming, Elena Karina, Adrian Saxe); USA; ca. 1980.
small collection of earthenware and stoneware objects (including pieces by Maria Martinez, David Shaner, Marguerite Wildenhain); USA; 20th century.

Costume (Garments and Accessories)
3 dresses, design attributed to Coco Chanel; Paris; ca. 1910.
75 fans; England, France; 18th and 19th centuries.

Enamel
150 enamel boxes, étuis, tea caddies; England; 18th and 19th centuries.
small collection of enameled religious artifacts; Limoges; 13th century.

Furniture
200 pieces of furniture; Europe, USA; 16th through 20th centuries.
150 pieces of furniture; Europe; ca. 1890.
small collection from an exhibition of moderately priced furniture (including pieces of plastic and wood); USA; ca. 1970.
small collection of cast-iron garden furniture; USA; mid-and late-19th century.

Glass

200 glass fragments, jewelry items, ornaments, and vessels; China, Egypt, Syria; 7th through 18th centuries.

small collection of lampwork scenes; Nevres; 17th century.

Jewelry

small collection of ancient jewelry; ceramic, bronze, glass, gold; China, Egypt, Italy; 4th century B.C. to 2nd century A.D.

50 dress ornaments, 19 of which comprise a set; enameled gold; Italy or Germany; 16th century.

small collection of jewelry; Austria, Germany, Italy; 16th century.

small collection of jewelry (including pieces by Maubossin Workshop, Mellerio dits Meller); Paris; late 19th and early 20th centuries.

small collection of jewelry of precious and nonprecious materials (including pieces by Alexander Calder, Margaret de Patta, Louis Brent Kington, Ronald Pearson; USA; 20th century.

Lighting Devices

small collection of candlesticks, chandeliers, lamps, and wall lamps (including objects by Louis Chalon, Louchet, Paul Manship, Quezal, Tiffany Studios); England, France; USA; late 19th and early 20th centuries.

Machinery and Tools

set of engraver's tools; France; mid-19th century.

Metalwork: Base Metals

small collection of bronze vessels; China; 15th to 10th centuries B.C.

stainless steel salt and pepper shakers by Charles Sheeler; USA; 20th century.

small collection of iron hardware; France; 15th century.

Metalwork: Precious Metals

gold flask; China; 15th century.

small collection of silver and silver-plated tablewares; Europe, USA; late 19th and early 20th centuries.

Other Materials

small collection of carved ivory religious objects; Europe; 12th through 16th centuries.

small collection of emerald, jade, marble objects (including figures, ornaments, vessels); China, India, Iran; 10th through 17th centuries.

pair of alabaster carvings attributed to the Nottingham school; England; early to mid-15th century.

small collection of wood carvings; Austria, England, Germany; 15th and 16th centuries.

small collection of wooden bowls (including works by Mark Lindquist, James Prestini); USA; late 20th century.

Textiles

small collection of rugs; China, India, Turkey; early 20th century.

small collection of tapestries; Flanders; mid-19th century.

small collection of textiles by contemporary fiber artists (including works by Lia Cook, Shelia Hicks, Gerhardt Knodel, Sherri Smith); USA; 20th century.

FINDING AIDS
Computerized catalog of the decorative arts in the collection.

SELECTED PUBLICATIONS
Herman, Lloyd E. *American Porcelain: New Expressions in an Ancient Art*. Forest Grove, Oregon: Timber Press, 1980.
Catalog of this juried exhibition contains illustrations of the 108 selected objects. Approximately forty of these contemporary porcelain works are in the Museum's collection.

LENDING POLICY
Loans are made to other institutions or galleries for public display and special exhibitions. Loans are not made to private individuals. All loan requests must be in writing, addressed to the Museum Director. Procedure for an approved loan will be administered through the Office of the Registrar, National Museum of American Art.

PHOTODUPLICATION SERVICE
Available at prevailing rates, subject to rules and procedures of the Museum. Requests should include accession numbers and be addressed to the Office of Visual Resources, National Museum of American Art.

PUBLIC ACCESS
Galleries are open from 10–5:30 daily except Christmas. Research inquiries and requests for access to objects not currently on exhibition should be addressed to the

Office of the Registrar
National Museum of American Art
Smithsonian Institution
Washington, D.C. 20560

8

National Museum of American History

The mission of the National Museum of American History is to illuminate the history of the United States and the influences which have shaped our national character. The history and development of the American nation—her communities and culture, her scientific and technological growth, along with her economic, social, and national history—are represented in the Museum's collections. The Museum is interested in how these objects were made and used, how they express human needs and values, and how they influence American society and the lives of individuals. Additionally, objects are studied as expressions of human creativity.

The rich and varied collections of the National Museum of American History contain objects which were made and/or used in this country—from 17th century archeological artifacts to 20th century atom smashers, from musical instruments to military equipment, from samplers to stamps, from washing machines to White House memorabilia. Some of these holdings, which were originally part of the Smithsonian Institution's ethnological collections, were augmented by the acquisition of numerous objects assembled for the 1876 Centennial Exposition in Philadelphia, as well as the transferal of selected patent models from the Patent Office in 1908 and in 1926.

In 1955 Congress authorized the construction of the Museum, which was designed by McKim, Meade and White and opened to the public in 1964.

23

24 Water cooler, ca. 1825–35.
    Mid-Atlantic, USA.
    Salt-glazed stoneware with incised and
    cobalt-filled decoration.

23 "Dove of Peace" pin designed by René
    Lalique for Mrs. Woodrow Wilson,
    presented to her by the people of Paris
    when she accompanied her husband to
    the Paris Peace Conference, 1918.

8A

Collection of Business Americana

The Smithsonian Institution Collection of Business Americana is concerned with the history of American business and advertising, principally from 1860 to 1940. The extensive Isadore Warshaw Collection acquired by the National Museum of American History in the late 1960s forms the core of this unique collection which includes advertisements, bills, catalogs, directories, price lists, receipts, and other items relating to all types of American enterprise. Holdings are rich in printed material pertaining to the decorative arts and represent the clothing, furniture, textile, and silver industries, among others.

While archival materials constitute the majority of the collection, there are holdings of three-dimensional objects: ceramic, glass, and metal containers, and textile sample books, which portray advertising and/or packaging techniques used in the United States.

FINDING AIDS
A Finding Guide to the Collection is available for use in the collection area.
The collection is arranged by subject (e.g., agriculture, furniture, silver, etc.).
Approximately half of the collection is indexed by manufacturer within each subject classification.
Three-dimensional materials are arranged by subject but not indexed.

LENDING POLICY
Loans are granted to educational institutions. Loans must be approved by the Archivist and are subject to review by the Collections Committee of the National Museum of American History. An information sheet is available from the Office of the Registrar, National Museum of American History.

PHOTODUPLICATION SERVICE
Available at prevailing rates, subject to rules and procedures of the Archivist of the Archives Center and the Museum. Inquiries should be addressed to the Offices of Printing and Photographic Services, National Museum of American History.

PUBLIC ACCESS
Exhibition galleries open from 10–5:30 daily except Christmas. Museum hours may be extended between Memorial Day and Labor Day. Research inquiries and requests for information concerning objects not currently on exhibition write to the Archivist, Archives Center
National Museum of American History
Smithsonian Institution
Washington, D.C. 20560

8B

Division of Ceramics and Glass

The Division of Ceramics and Glass is concerned primarily with ceramic and glass artifacts made and/or used in America. The collection includes approximately 16,000 examples of Western ceramics dating from the 16th century to the present. There are, in addition, Chinese and Japanese porcelains made for the Western market. The policy of the Division is not to collect classical, pre-Columbian, American Indian, or Oriental ceramics other than export wares. The approximately 6,000-object glass collection is strongest in 19th century American material. Glass holdings also include ancient glass as well as 18th and 19th century pieces from England and continental Europe.

The outstanding Hans Syz Collection documents the development of European porcelain manufacture during the 18th century, with particular emphasis on the factories at Meissen and Vienna. A significant aspect of the collection is the assemblage of "comparison porcelains" which trace the influence of Chinese and Japanese decorative motifs on their 18th century European counterparts.

The acquisition of several major collections of traditional American earthenware, stoneware, and art pottery has resulted in these areas ranking among the best in this country. Stoneware collections comprise the John P. Remensnyder, Robert Young Brown, and Cornelius Osgood collections. The important and comprehensive Remensnyder Collection contains late 18th to mid-19th century stoneware made in the northeastern United States; the Brown Collection focuses on 19th century northeastern manufacturers; and the Osgood Collection is concerned almost exclusively with stoneware from Bennington, Vermont. Holdings of American earthenware include the Lura Woodside Watkins Collection of 18th and 19th century New England wares and archeological materials from New England kiln sites. Also, there is a unique group of potter's tools made and used during the 19th century by the Thompson family of Morgantown, West Virginia, along with representative pieces of the pottery's production. American art pottery holdings, particularly strong in Rookwood examples, are composed primarily of the Marcus Benjamin Collection and Mrs. Page Kirk Collection. Commercial tablewares from late 19th and early 20th century American factories are well represented in the Benjamin Collection.

Holdings of English ceramics include the Mr. and Mrs. Jack Leon Collection of early 19th century yellow-glazed earthenware; the Clare Shenehon Boyd Collection of late 18th and early 19th century English tablewares; the Robert H. McCauley and Ellouise Baker Larsen collections of late 18th and 19th century transfer-printed pottery decorated with American views; Castleford-type; and lusterware pieces; and 18th century porcelain.

Additional ceramic collections include the E. Stanley Wires Collection of 18th through 20th century American and European tiles; a selection of ceramic items from the 1876 Centennial Exposition; the Wiley T. Buchanan Collection of

15th through 19th century Dutch and German earthenware and stoneware; and the Alfred Duanne Pell Collection representing 18th through 20th century European porcelain factories.

Among the Division's glass holdings are the Alma E. Duckworth Collection of American lamps, candlesticks, and tablewares, including many examples of lacy pressed glass and an important group of cup plates and salt dishes; the Preston Bassett Collection of American glass lighting devices, primarily from the 19th century; and 19th and 20th century pressed pattern glass from the Roger P. Templin Collection. A diverse collection containing mainly 19th century American, English, and continental European glass is contained in the Clara W. Berwick Collection. The Florence E. Bushee Collection of 19th and 20th century American and European paperweights contains especially fine French examples. Also in the American collections are Carder-Steuben glass given by Dr. and Mrs. Laverne G. Wagner; a group of Favrile glass selected by Louis Comfort Tiffany for the Smithsonian; cut and engraved glass; and six very rare examples of glass produced at the 18th century Frederick, Maryland, glassworks of John Frederick Amelung.

CLASSIFIED CATALOG OF OBJECTS

Ceramics

200 pipes; England, continental Europe, USA; 17th through 20th centuries.

1,700 tiles and tile panels; England, continental Europe, Middle East, USA; 18th through 20th centuries.

1,300 earthenware and stoneware utilitarian vessels; USA; 18th through 19th centuries.

small collection of African-American stoneware face vessels; USA; 19th century.

1,000 commercial tablewares; eastern and midwestern USA; 19th and early 20th centuries.

600 pieces of art pottery; USA; late 19th and early 20th centuries.

50 pieces of studio pottery; USA; 20th century.

3,400 earthenware figures and tablewares; England; 18th and 19th centuries.

2,000 porcelain figures and tablewares; England; mid-18th through 20th centuries.

5,000 earthenware and porcelain figures and tablewares; continental Europe; 18th through 20 centuries.

400 earthenware and stoneware utilitarian vessels; continental Europe; 15th through 19th centuries.

400 porcelain tablewares; China, Japan, primarily for the Western market; 18th and 19th centuries.

Glass

200 ancient and Islamic glass vessels; Near East and other areas of early manufacture; 15th century B.C. through 13th century A.D.

525 glass vessels, decorative objects, and tablewares; Asia, primarily continental Europe; 18th through 20th centuries, a few earlier examples.

900 tablewares and utilitarian and decorative objects; England; 18th through 20th centuries, a few earlier examples.

375 blown glass and mold-blown vessels, tablewares, and lighting devices; USA; late 18th through 20th centuries.

1,500 lacy pressed glass tablewares and lighting devices; USA; ca. 1830–40.

1,450 press-molded glass decorative objects, lighting devices, and tablewares; USA; mid-19th through early 20th centuries.

350 art glass objects; USA; late 19th and early 20th centuries.

100 figural flasks; USA; 19th century.

275 paperweights; China, England, continental Europe, USA; 19th and 20th centuries (primarily 19th century French).

150 cut glass and engraved glass tablewares and decorative objects; USA; late 19th through 20th centuries.

150 depression glass tablewares; USA; ca. 1930s.

25 contemporary studio glass objects; USA; mid-20th century.

FINDING AIDS

Card catalog arranged by catalog number.

Supplementary card catalog and indexes of the Leon and Pell collections.

SELECTED PUBLICATIONS

Gardner, Paul Vickers. *Meissen and Other German Porcelain in the Alfred Duanne Pell Collection*. Washington, D.C.: National Museum of History and Technology, 1956.

Brief histories of the factories including marks of the Meissen, Berlin, Frankenthal, Furstenberg, Hochst, Kloster-Veilsdorf, Ludwigsburg, Nymphenburg, and Vienna factories are given. A selected number of pieces are illustrated, all are described, and a chronological chart of the German porcelain factories represented in the Pell Collection is given.

Larsen, Ellouise Baker. *American Historical Views on Staffordshire China*. Garden City, N. Y.: Doubleday & Co., 1939.

This is the standard reference book on American historical views on Staffordshire pottery. The wares, potters, artists, and forms are included in the text. Most of the 795 illustrated pieces are now in the Division's collection.

McCauley, Robert H. *Liverpool Transfer Designs on Anglo-American Pottery*. Portland, Maine: Southworth-Anthoensen Press, 1942.

This volume attempts to classify and enlarge the known lists of designs on Liverpool ware which relate to both American trade and history. Designs are discussed according to subjects. Includes a descriptive checklist of transfer designs.

Miller, J. Jefferson, II. *Eighteenth Century English Porcelain: A Brief Guide to the Collection in the National Museum of History and Technology*. Washington, D.C.: Smithsonian Institution Press, 1973.

This illustrated guide to some of the more interesting pieces in the collection provides brief histories of the early English porcelain factories. Includes descriptions and illustrations of selected examples, also a bibliography.

———. *English Yellow-Glazed Earthenware*. Washington, D.C.: Smithsonian Institution Press, 1974.

The first major study of late 18th and early 19th century yellow-glazed earthenware, this volume is based on the collection now in the Division and assembled by Mr. and Mrs. Jack Leon. Decorations, forms, manufacturers, and views are discussed. Approximately seventy-four pieces are illustrated.

Myers, Susan H. *The John Paul Remensnyder Collection of American Stoneware.* Washington, D.C.: National Museum of History and Technology, 1978.

This essay describes the strengths of the Remensnyder Collection of traditional stoneware made in the northeastern United States. Illustrations of ten of the most important pieces in this collection.

Osgood, Cornelius. *The Jug and Related Stoneware of Bennington.* Rutland, Vt.: Charles E. Tuttle Co., 1971.

This volume discusses the technical aspects of ceramics, pottery-making in New England, the Nortons of Bennington, and their productions, along with comparisons with the products of other kilns. Glossary of terms, genealogical chart, description of marks, and bibliography included. Most of the pieces in the sixty-six illustrations are now in the Division.

Syz, Hans; Miller, J. Jefferson, II; Rückert, Rainer. *Catalogue of The Hans Syz Collection: Meissen Porcelain and Hausmalerei, Volume I.* Washington, D.C.: Smithsonian Institution Press, 1980.

This study of Meissen's early years uses pieces from the collection to illustrate the evolution of form and decoration. The catalog is organized roughly chronologically and according to decorative subject and technique. Individual entries contain descriptions of each piece along with detailed historical and technical information. Illustrations of 400 objects in the collection.

Watkins, Lura Woodside. *Early New England Potters and Their Wares.* Cambridge, Mass.: Harvard University Press, 1950.

This volume discusses forms and techniques in New England Pottery from the 17th through the 19th century. Documents relating to the Parkers of Charlestown, a checklist of New England potters, and a bibliography are included. A description, marks, origin, date, and measurements accompany the 136 illustrations of pieces, most of which are in the Division's holdings.

Wires, E. Stanley. "Decorative Tiles: Their Contribution to Architecture and Ceramic Art." *New England Architect and Builder, Illustrated* 14, pp. 12–22; No. 15, pp. 9–18; No. 16, pp. 15–26; No. 17, pp. 21–31 (1960).

These four monographs discuss the development of ceramic tiles from the ancient, medieval, and renaissance periods up to the present. The Dutch, English, and American tile industries are included. There are numerous illustrations from the Division's Wires Collection.

LENDING POLICY

Loans are granted to educational institutions for exhibition. Loans must be approved by the Curator and are subject to review by the Collections Committee of the National Museum of American History. An information sheet is available from the Office of the Registrar, National Museum of American History.

PHOTODUPLICATION SERVICE
Available at prevailing rates, subject to rules and procedures of the Division and the Museum. Inquiries should be addressed to the Office of Printing and Photographic Services, National Museum of American History.

PUBLIC ACCESS
Exhibition galleries open from 10–5:30 daily except Christmas. Museum hours may be extended between Memorial Day and Labor Day. Research inquiries and information concerning objects not currently on exhibition write to the

Division of Ceramics and Glass
National Museum of American History
Smithsonian Institution
Washington, D.C. 20560

8c

Division of Community Life

The Division of Community Life is concerned with everyday American communal activities and ethnic (non-Anglo and non-Indian) cultural practices. Holdings pertain to the history of sports, entertainment, community service organizations, labor, education, trades, and commercial establishments, as well as religious, ethnic, and regional groups. Although there is material from Europe and Latin America, the majority of the 12,000 objects relate to the study of American cultural history. The collections of European costume material; American and Latin American decorated horse gear; and European Roman Catholic, Judaic, and Orthodox material are particularly strong.

The Division also collects hand tools traditionally used by American artisans who worked in leather, metal, stone, and wood from the 17th century to the present. Due to the acquisition in 1977 of the John R. Gerwig, Jr., Collection of 1,200 tools used in the building trades, holdings are strongest in general woodworking tools dating from the second half of the 19th century. Particular emphasis is placed on acquiring sets of tools with known provenance.

CLASSIFIED CATALOG OF OBJECTS

Architectural Elements
small collection of carved wooden panels; Canada; late 19th century.
small collection of architectural elements from several churches; southwestern USA; 17th through 20th centuries.
school rooms; Mystic, Connecticut, and Cleveland, Ohio; ca. 1863 and 1886, respectively.

small collection of interior and exterior elements from several business establishments and a union hall (including a butcher shop, Automat, and confectionary); California, Philadelphia, Washington, D.C.: late 19th and early 20th centuries.

Basketry
50 basketry items; Africa, Europe, USA (including African-American); 20th century.

Ceramics
amphora decorated with sporting motifs; earthenware; Greece; ca. 510 B.C.

Costume (Garments and Accessories)
900 traditional costumes and accessories; Europe, Latin America; 19th and 20th centuries.

small collection of occupational uniforms (including cowboys' and firefighters'); France, Latin America, USA; late 19th and 20th centuries.

small collection of ceremonial, club, and organization costumes (including Boy and Girl Scouts, Campfire Girls, Masons); USA; 20th century.

small collection of embroidered religious vestments (including Catholic, Judaic, and Orthodox); Europe, Middle East; 17th through 20th centuries.

Furniture
small collection of furniture, made by members of ethnic groups; Canada, Europe, USA (Southwest and Pennsylvania); 18th through 20th centuries.

100 furniture patent models for school desks; USA; ca. 1860–98.

Jewelry
50 pieces of jewelry; silver; Europe, Latin America; 19th and 20th centuries.

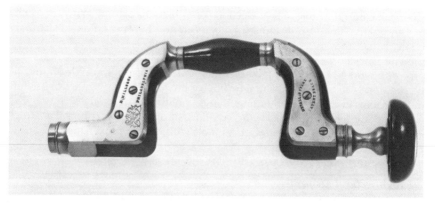

25 Cabinetmaker's brace, late nineteenth century.
Made in England for the E. Mills Company, Philadelphia, Pennsylvania.
Ebony and brass.

Metalwork: Base Metals
100 brass, bronze, and copper (some enameled) icons; eastern Europe, Russia; 17th through 20th centuries.
30 brass, copper, and iron household utensils; Europe; 16th through 20th centuries.
small collection of gold and silver Judaica; Europe, Middle East; 19th and 20th centuries.
small collection of silver Roman Catholic artifacts; Canada, Mexico; 19th century.
small collection of silver household artifacts; Canada, Europe, Latin America; 17th through 20th centuries.

Other Materials
30 decorated eggs and 170 watercolor designs for decorated eggs; eastern Europe; late 19th and 20th centuries.
50 carved ivory icons, figures, and triptychs; Europe; late 19th century.
50 pieces of leather horse gear (some with tooled leather and ornamented metal mountings); Latin America, USA; 18th through 20th centuries.
30 carved wooden Roman Catholic religious artifacts; Canada, Europe, Latin America; 19th and 20th centuries.
small collection of carved wooden icons; Europe; late 19th century.

Textiles
examples of fabric; Nigeria; ca. 1887.

Toys and Games
55 puppets, most used for American professional entertainment (including finger, hand, marionette, rod, and ventriloquist's figures); France, Italy, primarily USA; one 15th century, 19th and 20th centuries (primarily 20th century American).

FINDING AIDS
Card catalog arranged by accession number.
Partial supplementary subject indexes, subindexed by object type.
Hand tool collection indexed by trade.
Partial maker's name index.

SELECTED PUBLICATIONS
Welsh, Peter C. *Woodworking Tools, 1600–1900*. Contributions from the Museum of History and Technology, no. 51. Washington, D.C.: Smithsonian Institution Press, 1966.
Discusses the change in woodworking tools. Approximately twenty tools from the collection are illustrated.

LENDING POLICY
Loans are granted to educational institutions for exhibition. Loans must be approved by the Curator and are subject to review by the Collections Committee of the National Museum of American History. An information sheet is available from the Office of the Registrar, National Museum of American History.

PHOTODUPLICATION SERVICE
Available at prevailing rates, subject to rules and procedures of the Division and the Museum. Inquiries should be addressed to the Office of Printing and Photographic Services, National Museum of American History.

PUBLIC ACCESS
Exhibition galleries open from 10–5:30 daily except Christmas. Museum hours may be extended between Memorial Day and Labor Day. Research inquiries and information concerning objects not currently on exhibition write to the

Division of Community Life
National Museum of American History
Smithsonian Institution
Washington, D.C. 20560

8D

Division of Costume

The Division of Costume is concerned with the objects documenting the appearance of Americans as an expression of economic, social, and technological changes. In particular, the Division focuses on the typical appearance of non-Indian civilians of all socio-economic levels living within the territory of the United States during the last three centuries.

The collection contains approximately 22,000 garments and accessories worn by men, women, and children from the 17th century to the present day with strongest holdings in women's late 19th century clothing and jewelry. Holdings also include a unique collection of American objects used in the manufacturing and selling of clothing from the 19th century to the present. Such items include measuring and drafting devices used by tailors and dressmakers to draft patterns for the custom-made trade; pressing, pleating, and cutting devices; patent models; and original store mannequins and display forms.

There are two cohesive yet varied collections of particular interest to costume historians. The first, the collection of the Copp family of Stonington, Connecticut, consists of 275 items and is particularly strong in everyday clothing from the late 18th and early 19th centuries. The second, the designer collection, contains approximately 600 items by 20th century American and foreign designers who have significantly influenced American fashion, for example Adrian, Claire McCardell, and Norell.

CLASSIFIED CATALOG OF OBJECTS

Costume (Garments and Accessories)
4,400 men's, women's, and children's garments (including outerwear and un-

derwear for all occasions); primarily made or used in the USA; 17th century to the present day.

accessories used for the care of the body including compacts, cosmetic and hair care items, patches, and wigs; used in the USA; 19th and 20th centuries.

8,000 accessories including card cases, fans, footwear, hair ornaments, handwear, headware, neckwear, purses; USA; 18th century to the present day.

Jewelry

4,000 pieces of jewelry ranging from watches to shoe buckles; celluloid, coral, enamel, glass, gold, rolled gold, paste, silver, tortoiseshell; Europe, USA; 18th century to the present.

FINDING AIDS

Card catalog arranged by catalog number.

Indexes of designers, makers, and sellers.

Indexes of garment and accessory type arranged by form, subindexed by sex and century.

SELECTED PUBLICATIONS

Kidwell, Claudia B. *Women's Bathing and Swimming Costume in the United States.* United States National Museum Bulletin 250. Washington, D.C.: Smithsonian Institution Press, 1968.

This publication traces the evolution of the modern swim suit from colonial times to the present, noting changes in women's aquatic activities and in fashion, as well as changes in attitudes and the status of women in the United States. Includes illustrations of articles in the collection.

Kidwell, Claudia B., and Christman, Margaret C. *Suiting Everyone: The Democratization of Clothing in America.* Washington, D.C.: Smithsonian Institution Press, 1974.

This publication discusses and traces the historical and technological revolution in the making of clothing (from homemade to factory-made), as well as the revolution in wearing clothing (from the clothing of a class and occupation to a country where many persons dress alike).

Kidwell, Claudia B. *Cutting a Fashionable Fit: Dressmakers' Drafting Systems in the United States.* Smithsonian Institution Studies in History and Technology, no. 42. Washington, D.C.: Smithsonian Institution Press, 1979.

This important volume documents the development of dressmakers' drafting systems which were necessary to make late 19th century women's clothing fit properly. The book also discusses the economic, social, and technological factors which affected clothing construction techniques. In addition it describes how drafting systems were sold, and who used them.

LENDING POLICY

Loans are granted to educational institutions for exhibition. Loans must be approved by the Curator and are subject to review by the Collections Committee of the National Museum of American History. An information sheet is available from the Office of the Registrar, National Museum of American History.

PHOTODUPLICATION SERVICE

Available at prevailing rates, subject to rules and procedures of the Division and the Museum. Inquiries should be addressed to the Office of Printing and Photographic Services, National Museum of American History.

PUBLIC ACCESS

Exhibition galleries open from 10–5:30 daily except Christmas. Museum hours may be extended between Memorial Day and Labor Day. Research inquiries and information concerning objects not currently on exhibition write to the

Division of Costume
National Museum of American History
Smithsonian Institution
Washington, D.C. 20560

8E

Division of Domestic Life

The Division of Domestic Life is concerned with artifacts and activities relating to the American home from the 17th century to the present. The principal categories of the 30,000 object collection, the majority of which is American in origin, are furniture, small woodenwares, architecture, metalwares, and lighting devices. While this material includes decorative arts of high quality, many of the artifacts are representative of types used by the middle class.

The Division has a number of notable collections. Among these is one of the largest assemblages of lighting devices in this country, primarily donated by Preston R. Bassett and by Virgil Hillyer. The John Paul Remensynder Collection of brass and copper objects is particularly rich in marked examples of coppersmiths' work. Included in the Joseph Kler Collection of Pewter (on indefinite loan to the Division) are rare American pieces. The range of types of European pewter liquid measures are illustrated in the W. Gill Wylie Collection. The Charles F. Wiebusch Collection comprises a large group of cutlery and flatware. Silver objects of 18th and early 19th century origin constitute the Arthur V. Michaels Collection. The Leo Stoor Collection of smoking equipment contains a sizable selection of decorative meerschaum pipes and cigar holders. A major portion of the collection of New England household furnishings donated to the museum by Dr. and Mrs. Arthur Greenwood is located in this Division. There are, in addition, a number of collections of artifacts which have descended in families, for example, those of the Copp family of Stonington, Connecticut, and the Ramsay family of Alexandria, Virginia.

CLASSIFIED CATALOG OF OBJECTS

Architectural Elements

interior and exterior elements from 16 houses of known origin and date; USA, primarily from the East Coast; late 17th through 20th centuries.

small collection of architectural fragments and hardware; USA; 17th through 20th centuries.

Basketry

50 baskets; USA, primarily New England and Appalachia; 19th century and 20th centuries.

Bibelots and Miniatures

475 cigar, cigarette, match, and snuff boxes and cases; primarily brass, papier-mâché, silver; Great Britain, USA; 18th through 20th centuries.

small collection of doll houses and doll house furnishings; primarily USA; late 19th and early 20th centuries.

Furniture

530 pieces of household furniture, primarily chairs; USA; 17th through 20th centuries.

30 patent models for furniture; USA; ca. 1860–1900.

Heating Devices

small collection of cast-iron firebacks, stoves, and stove plates; USA; 19th century.

Lighting Devices

4,000 lighting devices and related objects including candlesticks, candle molds, chandeliers, firemaking apparatus, lamps, lanterns, matchsafes, patent models, rush holders, snuffers, trimmers; brass, iron, pewter, tin-plated sheet iron, wood; Europe, primarily USA; 17th through 20th centuries.

Metalwork: Base Metals

300 bell metal, brass, copper cooking utensils and pieces of fireplace equipment; USA; 18th and 19th centuries.

475 pieces of pewter (including more than 250 liquid measures); Europe, USA; 18th and 19th centuries.

875 tin-plated sheet iron household implements and containers, 60 examples decoratively painted; primarily USA; primarily 19th century.

small collection of enameled sheet iron household implements; primarily USA; late 19th and early 20th century.

250 pieces of iron fireplace equipment and cooking utensils; USA; 18th and 19th centuries.

Metalwork: Precious Metals

2,500 pieces of silver and silver-plated flatware and hollow ware; primarily USA; 17th through 20th centuries.

Other Materials

100 bone, horn, and ivory household utensils and ornamental objects; USA;

primarily 19th century.

100 woodenwares; USA; eighteenth and nineteenth centuries.

Textiles

75 miscellaneous curtains, draperies, trimmings, and valances; USA; 19th century.

FINDING AIDS

Card catalog arranged by catalog number.

Maker's index arranged alphabetically by maker's name or mark.

SELECTED PUBLICATIONS

Hough, Walter. *Collection of Heating and Lighting Utensils in the United States National Museum*. United States National Museum Bulletin, no. 141. Washington, D.C.: United States Government Printing Office, 1928.

Illustrated catalog of heating and lighting devices throughout the Smithsonian Institution. Many are in the Division of Domestic Life.

Wylie, W. Gill. *Pewter: Measure for Measure*. Privately Printed, 1952.

Illustrated catalog of the Wylie Collection, now in the Division of Domestic Life.

LENDING POLICY

Loans are granted to educational institutions for exhibition. Loans must be approved by the Curator and are subject to review by the Collections Committee of the National Museum of American History. An information sheet is available from the Office of the Registrar, National Museum of American History.

PHOTODUPLICATION SERVICE

Available at prevailing rates, subject to rules and procedures of the Division and the Museum. Inquiries should be addressed to the Office of Printing and Photographic Services, National Museum of American History.

PUBLIC ACCESS

Exhibition galleries open from 10–5:30 daily except Christmas. Museum hours may be extended between Memorial Day and Labor Day. Research inquiries and information concerning objects not currently on exhibition write to the

Division of Domestic Life
National Museum of American History
Smithsonian Institution
Washington, D.C. 20560

8F

Division of Electricity and Modern Physics

The Division of Electricity and Modern Physics is concerned with the development of electricity and modern physics including specialized fields such as electrical motors, electrostatics, generators, meters, radio, telegraphy, and television. Holdings of approximately 14,000 objects including patent models date from 1830 to the present and are of American and European origin.

CLASSIFIED CATALOG OF OBJECTS

Architectural Elements
telephone booth; USA; ca. 1890.

Furniture
small collection of loudspeakers, radios, televisions, with decorative cabinets or ornamental features; USA; late 19th and 20th centuries.

FINDING AIDS
Card catalog arranged by subject, subindexed by catalog number.

LENDING POLICY
Loans are granted to educational institutions for exhibition. Loans must be approved by the curator and are subject to review by the Collections Committee of the National Museum of American History. An information sheet is available from the Office of the Registrar, National Museum of American History.

PHOTODUPLICATION SERVICE
Available at prevailing rates, subject to rules and procedures of the Division and the Museum. Inquiries should be addressed to the Office of Printing and Photographic Services, National Museum of American History.

PUBLIC ACCESS
Exhibition galleries open from 10–5:30 daily except Christmas. Museum hours may be extended between Memorial Day and Labor Day. Research inquiries and information concerning objects not currently on exhibition write to the

Division of Electricity and Modern Physics
National Museum of American History
Smithsonian Institution
Washington, D.C. 20560

8G

Division of Extractive Industries

The Division of Extractive Industries is concerned with American agriculture, including plant and animal husbandry and the forestry, fishing, mining, mineral, and food technology industries, from the 18th century to the present. Objects related to agricultural production (defined as processes performed on raw materials on the farm) and agricultural processing (defined as processes performed on raw materials after they have left the farm) are held by the Division. The collection also contains hand tools and patent models which pertain to these industries.

CLASSIFIED CATALOG OF OBJECTS

Costume (Garments and Accessories)
50 pairs of leather shoes; Asia, Europe; early 20th century.
60,000 buttons of a variety of materials; Europe, USA; 18th through 20 centuries.
1,400 walking sticks collected as wood samples but with decorated handles; various origins and dates.
small collection of walking stick handles; carved bone; USA; late 19th and early 20th centuries.

Metalwork: Base Metals
300 tin candy and ice cream molds; Europe, primarily USA; late 19th through mid-20th centuries.

Other Materials
small collection of ornamented bone, horn, and ivory objects (including combs, pie crimpers, figures, walking stick handles); USA; late 19th and early 20th centuries.
small collection of tooled leather saddles; USA; ca. 1835.

FINDING AIDS

Card Catalog arranged by accession number.
Three indexes, one each for agricultural processes, agricultural production, and mineral industries.
Each index arranged by major subject, subindexed by types of object and catalog number.

LENDING POLICY

Loans are granted to educational institutions for exhibition. Loans must be approved by the Curator and are subject to review by the Collections Committee of the National Museum of American History. An information sheet is available from the Office of the Registrar, National Museum of American History.

PHOTODUPLICATION SERVICE
Available at prevailing rates, subject to rules and procedures of the Division and the Museum. Inquiries should be addressed to the Office of Printing and Photographic Services, National Museum of American History.

PUBLIC ACCESS
Exhibition galleries open from 10–5:30 daily except Christmas. Museum hours may be extended between Memorial Day and Labor Day. Research inquiries and information concerning objects not currently on exhibition write to the

Division of Extractive Industries
National Museum of American History
Smithsonian Institution
Washington, D.C. 20560

8H

Division of Graphic Arts

The Division of Graphic Arts is concerned with the technical history of printing and the allied trades. Holdings comprise prints, drawings, and photomechanical prints (totaling approximately 43,500 items), printing presses, type, and founding materials, as well as bookbinding and papermaking tools. The Columbian and Firefly presses are particularly notable examples of ornamented iron castings. For a complete description of the print collection, see the *Finders' Guide to Prints and Drawings in the Smithsonian Institution* by Lynda C. Claassen.

FINDING AIDS
Card catalog arraged by catalog and accession numbers, makers, and donors. Subject file for part of the print collection.

LENDING POLICY
Loans are granted to educational institutions for exhibition. Loans must be approved by the Curator and are subject to review by the Collections Committee of the National Museum of American History. An information sheet is available from the Office of the Registrar, National Museum of American History.

PHOTODUPLICATION SERVICE
Available at prevailing rates, subject to rules and procedures of the Division and the Museum. Inquiries should be addressed to the Office of Printing and Photographic Services, National Museum of American History.

PUBLIC ACCESS
Exhibition galleries open from 10–5:30 daily except Christmas. Museum hours

may be extended between Memorial Day and Labor Day. Research inquiries and information concerning objects not currently on exhibition write to the

Division of Graphic Arts
National Museum of American History
Smithsonian Institution
Washington, D.C. 20560

8I

Division of Mathematics

The Division of Mathematics is concerned with the development of computation, data processing, geometry, logic, and measurement, along with dividing and ruling engines. Although American-made devices are emphasized, western European instruments which were used in this country or which served as prototypes are included in this 10,000-object collection. Holdings are particularly strong in postdigital computing devices and geometric models.

CLASSIFIED CATALOG OF OBJECTS
Timekeeping and Measuring Devices
small collection of astrolabes, sundials, and sectors, many of elaborately engraved brass; Europe; 16th through 19th centuries.

FINDING AIDS
Computerized index of entire collection.

LENDING POLICY
Loans are granted to educational institutions for exhibition. Loans must be approved by the Curator and are subject to review by the Collections Committee of the National Museum of American History. An information sheet is available from the Office of the Registrar, National Museum of American History.

PHOTODUPLICATION SERVICE
Available at prevailing rates, subject to rules and procedures of the Division and the Museum. Inquiries should be addressed to the Office of Printing and Photographic Services, National Museum of American History.

PUBLIC ACCESS
Exhibition galleries open from 10–5:30 daily except Christmas. Museum hours may be extended between Memorial Day and Labor Day. Research inquiries and

information concerning objects not currently on exhibition write to the

Division of Mathematics
National Museum of American History
Smithsonian Institution
Washington, D.C. 20560

8 J

Division of Mechanical and Civil Engineering

The Division of Mechanical and Civil Engineering is concerned with the history and development of civil engineering, production engineering, and power machinery in the United States. The collection contains a total of 5,000 full-size and model machines and machine tools.

CLASSIFIED CATALOG OF OBJECTS

Machinery and Tools
1,500 machines and machine tools, with metallic cast, stamped, worked and/or painted decorative elements; USA; ca. 1823–90.

FINDING AIDS
Card catalog arranged by catalog number.
Card catalog arranged by subject.

LENDING POLICY
Loans are granted to educational institutions for exhibition. Loans must be approved by the Curator and are subject to review by the Collections Committee of the National Museum of American History. An information sheet is available from the Office of the Registrar, National Museum of American History.

PHOTODUPLICATION SERVICE
Available at prevailing rates, subject to rules and procedures of the Division and the Museum. Inquiries should be addressed to the Office of Printing and Photographic Services, National Museum of American History.

PUBLIC ACCESS
Exhibition galleries open from 10–5:30 daily except Christmas. Museum hours may be extended between Memorial Day and Labor Day. Research inquiries and

information concerning objects not currently on exhibition write to the

Division of Mechanical and Civil Engineering
National Museum of American History
Smithsonian Institution
Washington, D.C. 20560

8K

Division of Mechanisms

The Division of Mechanisms is concerned with the historical and technological development of light machinery, mechanisms, and related tools. The 4,600-object collection encompasses American and European automata, clocks and watches, locks, phonographs, typewriters, and other mechanisms dating from the 16th through the 20th centuries. The works of many well-known and important craftsmen are herein represented, including William Bond, David Rittenhouse, and Simon and Benjamin Willard.

Two major collections are on extended loan to the Division. The James Arthur Collection contains more than 2,000 clocks and watches dating from the 17th to the 20th centuries. The Munson-Williams-Proctor Collection includes more than 200 European art watches (defined as highly decorated watches) dating from the 16th to the 20th centuries.

CLASSIFIED CATALOG OF OBJECTS

Machinery and Tools
more than 100 phonographs and typewriters, some with painted decoration; USA; late 19th and early 20th centuries.
250 brass and iron escutcheons, hinges, locks and keys, ornamented hardware and strong boxes; primarily Europe, USA; 16th through 20th centuries.

Timepieces and Measuring Devices
530 clocks including alarm, mantel, miniature, shelf, table, tall, traveling, and wall; Europe, Japan, USA; 17th to 20th centuries.
3,500 watches; Europe, USA; 19th and 20th centuries.
100 sundials, primarily brass and pewter; Europe, Japan, USA; 16th through 19th centuries.
a small collection of automata including 1 in the form of a monk; south Germany; 1570.
300 clock and watchmaker's tools; Europe, primarily USA; mid-18th to 20th centuries, primarily 19th century.

FINDING AIDS
Card catalog arranged by type of mechanism.

26 Pocket watch, ca. 1809–17.
Made by Luther Goddard, Shrews-
bury, Massachusetts.
Brass, gilt brass, silver case.

Watches arranged by country, maker if known, and catalog number.
Clocks arranged by country, type, and catalog number.
Phonographs indexed by manufacturer, subindexed by catalog number.
Typewriters arranged by manufacturer and catalog number.
Locks and keys arranged alphabetically by maker's name.
Makers' index is partial.

SELECTED PUBLICATIONS

Frankel, Tobia. *Timepieces: From Sundials to Atomic Clocks.* In the Smithsonian:
The National Museum of History and Technology. Washington, D.C.:
Smithsonian Institution Press, 1977.
This pamphlet briefly documents the technological development of time-
pieces through the Division's wide variety of clocks. Forty-six are illustrated
and described.
Hoover, Cynthia A. *Music Machines—American Style: A Catalogue of the Exhibition.*
Washington, D.C.: Smithsonian Institution, 1971.

This exhibition catalog surveys the development in America of musical machines, ranging from record players to juke boxes, emphasizing the ways in which science and invention have affected the performer and his audience. Illustrations include general data rather than technical descriptions.

LENDING POLICY
Loans are granted to other museums for exhibition. Loans must be approved by the Curator and are subject to review by the Collections Committee of the National Museum of American History. An information sheet is available from the Office of the Registrar, National Museum of American History.

PHOTODUPLICATION SERVICE
Available at prevailing rates, subject to rules and procedures of the Division and the Museum. Inquiries should be addressed to the Office of Printing and Photographic Services, National Museum of American History.

PUBLIC ACCESS
Exhibition galleries open from 10–5:30 daily except Christmas. Museum hours may be extended between Memorial Day and Labor Day. Research inquiries and information concerning objects not currently on exhibition write to the

Division of Mechanisms
National Museum of American History
Smithsonian Institution
Washington, D.C. 20560

8L

Division of Medical Sciences

The Division of Medical Sciences is concerned with the history of American dentistry, medicine, public health, and pharmacy. Approximately half of the Division's decorative arts holdings are on loan from the American Pharmaceutical Association. This large collection is entitled the Squibb Ancient Pharmacy, and it contains several hundred European drug containers and utencils dating from the 15th through the 19th centuries. Additionally, the Division holds a unique collection of 19th and 20th century medical furniture.

CLASSIFIED CATALOG OF OBJECTS

Architectural Elements
interiors of 2 apothecaries; Germany, USA; 15th and 19th centuries.

Ceramics
610 earthenware and porcelain drug containers, 40 invalid feeders and mortars

and pestles; Europe, USA; 15th through 19th centuries.

small collection of phrenological heads; England; mid to late 19th century.

Costume (Garments and Accessories)

1,900 pairs of eyeglasses, including some of celluloid and silver; Europe, USA; 18th through 20th centuries.

65 medical uniforms; USA; 19th and 20th centuries.

Furniture

small collection of common wooden side chairs; Europe; mid-18th century.

150 examples of medical furniture, including dental chairs, hospital furniture, and chairs designed to correct poor posture; USA; 19th and 20th centuries.

Glass

370 enamel-decorated glass drug containers; Europe, primarily Germany, USA; 17th through 20th centuries.

610 reverse painted glass bottles and jars; Europe, USA; 19th and 20th centuries.

30 show globes (containers filled with colored liquid used as apothecary trade signs), some fitted with metal mountings; Europe, USA; 19th and 20th centuries.

31 reverse painted glass show jars (decorative containers used as apothecary trade signs); Europe, USA; 19th and 20th centuries.

Jewelry

silver tracheotomy necklace made by Mary Ann Scherr; USA; 1973.

Lighting Devices

small collection of iron, brass, and bronze candlesticks; Europe; 16th through 19th centuries.

Metalwork: Base Metals

115 bronze mortars and pestles; Europe; 15th through 19th centuries.

54 iron mortars and pestles; Europe, USA; 15th through 19th centuries.

20 sets of bronze nested weights; Europe, USA; 17th through 20th centuries.

50 brass, horn, and iron pan scales and weights; Europe, USA; 17th through 19th centuries.

Metalwork: Precious Metals

small collection of silver and gilt ear trumpets; England, Russia; 19th century.

Other Materials

60 agate, granite, lava, and marble mortars and pestles; Europe, Mexico; 7th through 19th centuries.

70 wooden mortars and drug containers; Europe; 17th through 19th centuries.

FINDING AIDS

Card catalog arranged by subject, subindexed by usage.

SELECTED PUBLICATIONS

Urdang, George, and Nitardy, F. W. *The Squibb Ancient Pharmacy: A Catalogue of the Collection.* New York: E. R. Squibb & Sons, 1940.

This illustrated catalog discusses the objects in the collection. More than half of the 1,102 catalog entries are illustrated.

LENDING POLICY
Loans are granted to educational institutions for exhibition. Loans must be approved by the Curator and are subject to review by the Collections Committee of the National Museum of American History. An information sheet is available from the Office of the Registrar, National Museum of American History.

PHOTODUPLICATION SERVICE
Available at prevailing rates, subject to rules and procedures of the Division and the Museum. Inquiries should be addressed to the Office of Printing and Photographic Services, National Museum of American History.

PUBLIC ACCESS
Exhibition galleries open from 10–5:30 daily except Christmas. Museum hours may be extended between Memorial Day and Labor Day. Research inquiries and information concerning objects not currently on exhibition write to the

Division of Medical Sciences
National Museum of American History
Smithsonian Institution
Washington, D.C. 20560

8M

Division of Military History

The Division of Military History is concerned primarily with the material aspects of American armed forces on land. The approximately 26,000 objects in this collection can be generally classified as uniforms, weapons, and related accessories. Most are American or European and date from the 17th century to the present.

The important weapon collection reflects the historical development of firearms and edged weapons. Of interest to decorative arts historians may be the comprehensive holdings of both presentation pieces and the gun as an art form (including the George Kennan, Ralph G. Packard, William G. Renwick, and Harry C. Knode Collections). A 15,000 item collection traces the stylistic development of uniforms, primarily of the U.S. Army, from about 1812 to the present. Holdings also include the comprehensive U.S. Army Quartermaster Corps Collection of Enlisted Uniforms, dating from 1833 to 1900, as well as those which were transferred from the U.S. War Department.

CLASSIFIED CATALOG OF OBJECTS

Arms and Armor

450 highly decorated presentation and miniature edged weapons and firearms; Europe, primarily USA; 17th through 20th centuries.

100 horns and metal powder horns and powder flasks primarily USA; mid-18th to mid-19th centuries.

Costume (Garments and Accessories)

15,000 U.S. Army, Militia, and National Guard Uniforms and accessories (including insignia, cap and belt plates); primarily USA, Europe; 1812 to present.

1,000 U.S. Army and Militia metal buttons; USA; ca. 1914 to present.

FINDING AIDS

Card catalog arranged alphabetically by donor.

Partial index by subject.

Supplementary catalog arranged by accession and catalog numbers.

SELECTED PUBLICATIONS

Belote, Theodore T. *American and European Swords in the Historical Collection of the United States National Museum*. Smithsonian Bulletin, no. 163. Washington, D.C.: Smithsonian Institution Press, 1932.

This catalog describes and documents the collection of swords. Many are illustrated.

Campbell, J. Duncan, and Howell, Edgar M. *American Military Insignia: 1850 to 1851*. Washington, D.C.: Smithsonian Institution Press, 1963.

The organization and insignia of both the regular Army and uniformed Militia are described. Cap and helmet devices, shoulder-belt and waist belt plates, primarily from the comprehensive W. Stokes Kirk Collection acquired in 1959, are cataloged.

Howell, Edgar M., and Kloster, Donald E. *United States Army Headgear to 1854: Catalog of United States Army Uniforms in the Collections of the Smithsonian Institution*. United States National Museum, Bulletin no. 269. Washington, D.C.: Smithsonian Institution Press, 1969.

Howell, Edgar. *United States Army Headgear 1855–1902: Catalog of United States Army Uniforms in the Smithsonian Collection*. Smithsonian Studies in History and Technology, no. 30. Washington, D.C.: Smithsonian Institution Press, 1975.

These 2 catalogs are designed to illustrate, describe, and document Army headgear in the collection. Most of the objects are from the comprehensive War Department Collection.

LENDING POLICY

Loans are granted to educational institutions for exhibition. Loans must be approved by the Curator and are subject to review by the Collections Committee of the National Museum of American History. An information sheet is available from the Office of the Registrar, National Museum of American History.

PHOTODUPLICATION SERVICE
Available at prevailing rates, subject to rules and procedures of the Division and the Museum. Inquiries should be addressed to the Office of Printing and Photographic Services, National Museum of American History.

PUBLIC ACCESS
Exhibition galleries open from 10–5:30 daily except Christmas. Museum hours may be extended between Memorial Day and Labor Day. Research inquiries and information concerning objects not currently on exhibition write to the

Division of Military History
National Museum of American History
Smithsonian Institution
Washington, D.C. 20560

8N

Division of Musical Instruments

The Division of Musical Instruments is concerned with all varieties of instruments used in the western world. Holdings of about 1,500 keyboard, mechanical, percussion, string, and wind instruments are of American (excluding native American, which are in the National Museum of Natural History) and Western European origin.

The core of this Division's important and comprehensive keyboard collection was donated by the late Hugo Worch, a Washington, D.C. piano dealer. Many of these instruments, significant both historically and artistically, are contained in highly decorated cases.

The collection of stringed instruments includes American and European pieces which are embellished with ebony, ivory, mother-of-pearl, and tortoise shell. Two exceptional carved examples are a bass *viola da gamba* by Barak Norman of London (1718) and a folk cello by George Jewett of New England made about 1795.

The wind instrument collection is primarily of 19th century American and European origin and is evenly divided between wood and brass examples. A decorated clarinet (basically a rosewood instrument but with silver keys, colored glass keytops, mother-of-pearl veneered barrel, jeweled rod, and inlaid silver eagle) made circa 1860 by Eisenbrandt of Baltimore, is outstanding.

Finally, there are small collections of both percussion and mechanical instruments. Notable examples are an important pair of drums (each mounted on a wrought iron stand) probably of German origin and made during the third quarter of the 18th century and a 1946 Wurlitzer Co. juke box—a bubbling kinetic sculpture.

CLASSIFIED CATALOG OF OBJECTS

Musical Instruments

260 keyboard instruments including clavichords, harpsichords, organs, and pianos; Europe, USA; late 17th through 20th centuries.

600 bowed and plucked string instruments including banjos, cellos, lutes, mandolins, violins, and violas; Europe; USA; 17th through 20th centuries.

550 brass and woodwinds; Europe, USA; primarily 19th century.

60 percussion instruments, primarily drums; Europe, USA; mid-18th century to present.

70 mechanical instruments including automata, barrel organs, music boxes and snuff boxes, player pianos; Europe, USA; 19th and 20th centuries.

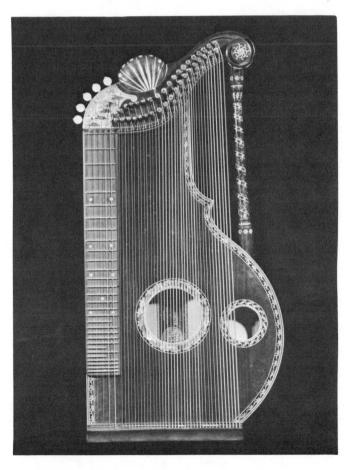

27   Zither, ca. 1890.
Made by Franz Schwarzer, Washington, Missouri.

FINDING AIDS

Card catalog arranged by catalog number.

Indexes arranged by type of instrument.

SELECTED PUBLICATIONS

Center, Durward R. *A Checklist of Mechanical Instruments in the Smithsonian Institution*, 1973.

This checklist includes fifty-two mechanical instruments and related items.

Division of Musical Instruments. *A Checklist of Keyboard Instruments in the Smithsonian Institution*, 1975.

This checklist includes 244 clavichords, organs, pianos, plucked stringed keyboards, and miscellaneous other instruments. Five of the Division's instruments are illustrated.

Eliason, Robert E. *Keyed Bugles in the United States*. Washington, D.C.: Smithsonian Institution Press, 1972.

This pamphlet traces the development of the keyed bugle. Five are illustrated.

Hollis, Helen Rice. *The Musical Instruments of Joseph Haydn: An Introduction*. Washington, D.C.: Smithsonian Institution Press, 1977.

This pamphlet describes 16 keyboard, percussion, and wind instruments used in Joseph Haydn's time.

———. *Pianos in the Smithsonian Institution*. Smithsonian Studies in History and Technology, no. 27. Washington, D.C.: Smithsonian Institution Press, 1973.

These seventeen American and European pianos represent important stages in the development of the modern piano from its earliest beginnings.

Hoover, Cynthia A. *Harpsichords and Clavichords*. Washington, D.C.: Smithsonian Institution Press, 1969.

This booklet describes and illustrates nine of the restored harpsichords and clavichords that are periodically on view and in use in the Hall of Musical Instruments.

———. *Music Machines—American Style: A Catalogue of the Exhibition*. Washington, D.C.: Smithsonian Institution Press, 1971.

This exhibition catalog surveys the development of musical machines in America emphasizing the ways in which science and invention have affected the performer and his audience. Illustrations include general data rather than technical descriptions.

Odell, J. Scott. *A Checklist of Banjos in the Collections of the Division of Musical Instruments, Smithsonian Institution*. 1971.

This checklist includes twenty-seven banjos.

———. *Plucked Dulcimers: A Checklist of Appalachian Dulcimers and Similar Instruments in the Collections of the Division of Musical Instruments, Smithsonian Institution*, 1971.

This checklist includes twenty plucked dulcimers and related instruments.

LENDING POLICY

Loans are granted to educational institutions for exhibition. Loans must be approved by the Curator and are subject to review by the Collections Committee of the National Museum of American History. An information sheet is available from the Office of the Registrar, National Museum of American History.

PHOTODUPLICATION SERVICE
Available at prevailing rates, subject to rules and procedures of the Division and the Museum. Inquiries should be addressed to the Office of Printing and Photographic Services, National Museum of American History.

PUBLIC ACCESS
Exhibition galleries open from 10–5:30 daily except Christmas. Museum hours may be extended between Memorial Day and Labor Day. Research inquiries and information concerning objects not currently on exhibition write to the

Division of Musical Instruments
National Museum of American History
Smithsonian Institution
Washington, D.C. 20560

80

Division of Naval History

The Division of Naval History is concerned with the history of the United States Navy as documented by objects, manuscripts, and illustrations. Collections include uniforms and their accessories, ship models, weapons, paintings, sketches, and a small number of presentation pieces, most dating from the nineteenth century to the present. The Division also holds a small collection of material from underwater sites in the Western Hemisphere, including ceramic, glass, and pewter items from the Revolutionary War ship the *Philadelphia*.

CLASSIFIED CATALOG OF OBJECTS

Arms and Armor
small collection of highly decorated presentation edged weapons and firearms; Europe, USA; 18th century to present.

Ceramics
2 pitchers (transfer printed Liverpool-type creamware depicting Stephen Decatur and Edward Preble); England; ca. 1810.

Costume (Garments and Accessories)
500 U.S. Coast Guard, Marine, Navy accessories and uniforms (including belts, decorations, epaulettes, headgear, and insignia); USA; from 1789 to the present.
100 military buttons; USA; 19th and 20th centuries.

needleworked Masonic apron presented to Admiral Winfield Scott Schley; USA; 1902.

Metalwork: Precious Metals
small collection of silver presentation pieces (including pieces by Dominick and Haff, Gorham, Maier and Beakele, and Towle); USA; late 19th and early 20th centuries.

FINDING AIDS
Card catalog arranged by donor.
Partial index by subject.

SELECTED PUBLICATIONS
Furlong, William Rea, and McCandless, Byron. *So Proudly We Hail: The History of the United States Flag*. Edited by Harold D. Langley. Washington, D.C.: Smithsonian Institution Press, 1981.
This volume documents the evolution of the American flag. Many different forms and media are illustrated: ceramics, textiles, paintings, drawings, and illustrations. All are datable, many are from the Division's collection.

LENDING POLICY
Loans are granted to educational institutions for exhibition. Loans must be approved by the Curator and are subject to review by the Collections Committee of the National Museum of American History. An information sheet is available from the Office of the Registrar, National Museum of American History.

PHOTODUPLICATION SERVICE
Available at prevailing rates, subject to rules and procedures of the Division and the Museum. Inquiries should be addressed to the Offices of Printing and Photographic Services, National Museum of American History.

PUBLIC ACCESS
Exhibition galleries open from 10–5:30 daily except Christmas. Museum hours may be extended between Memorial Day and Labor Day. Research inquiries and information concerning objects not currently on exhibition write to the

Division of Naval History
National Museum of American History
Smithsonian Institution
Washington, D.C. 20560

8P

Division of Photographic History

The Division of Photographic History is concerned with the applications and history of photography. Collections include historically and scientifically important apparatus, literature, and photographs associated with black-and-white still and motion picture photography. This material emphasizes the photographer, the technological processes, and the influences of photography on everyday life. Additionally, the Division holds approximately 1,000 American miniature photographic cases made of various materials, roughly 900 photographic cases of pressed synthetic material, and several hundred photographic albums of tooled and embossed leather.

CLASSIFIED CATALOG OF OBJECTS

Ceramics
small collection of tablewares with portrait affixed by a photographic process; France; ca. 1875.

Furniture
small collection of furniture from several photographic laboratories and studios; England, USA; mid-19th through early 20th centuries.

Machinery and Tools
small collection of early projection and viewing equipment with engraved, impressed, and painted metal parts; primarily USA; late 19th and early 20th centuries.

Other Materials
small collection of carved ivory souvenirs containing microphotographs; Europe; ca. 1890.

FINDING AIDS
Card catalog arranged by catalog number.
Partial indexes by equipment, image, maker, and process.

LENDING POLICY
Loans are granted to educational institutions for exhibition. Loans must be approved by the Curator and are subject to review by the Collections Committee of the National Museum of American History. An information sheet is available from the Office of the Registrar, National Museum of American History.

PHOTODUPLICATION SERVICE
Available at prevailing rates, subject to rules and procedures of the Division and the Museum. Inquiries should be addressed to the Office of Printing and Pho-

tographic Services, National Museum of American History.

PUBLIC ACCESS
Exhibition galleries open from 10–5:30 daily except Christmas. Museum hours may be extended between Memorial Day and Labor Day. Research inquiries and information concerning objects not currently on exhibition write to the

Division of Photographic History
National Museum of American History
Smithsonian Institution
Washington, D.C. 20560

8Q

Division of Physical Sciences

The Division of Physical Sciences is concerned with astronomical, chemical, metrological, meteorological, navigational, and surveying instrumentation, along with devices for teaching the general principles of science. The collection comprises approximately 6,000 objects including measuring devices and scientific apparatus, most of which were made and/or used in the United States. Of note is an air pump in an elaborately carved mahogany case made in the Boston-Salem area, ca. 1783. A special collection which documents the development of materials made of synthetic polymers includes clothing and jewelry of bakelite, celluloid, and other plastics.

CLASSIFIED CATALOG OF OBJECTS

Glass
small collection of glass chemical apparatus made for Joseph Priestly's laboratory (attributed to Josiah Wedgwood); England; late 18th century.

Timepieces and Measuring Devices
500 measuring devices and scientific apparatus, many with engraved or cast embellishments; primarily brass (makers include C. F. Brander, Goldsmith Chandlee, James Giles, David Rittenhouse); Europe, USA; late 18th and early 19th centuries.

FINDING AIDS
Card catalog arranged by accession number.
Indexes arranged by maker and discipline, subindexed by object type.

SELECTED PUBLICATIONS
Middleton, W. E. Knowles. *Catalog of Metrological Instruments in the Museum of*

History and Technology. Smithsonian Studies in History and Technology, no. 2. Washington, D.C.: Smithsonian Institution Press, 1969.
This illustrated paper catalogs the barometers, thermographs, thermometers, and other measuring devices in the collection.

LENDING POLICY
Loans are granted to educational institutions for exhibition. Loans must be approved by the Curator and are subject to review by the Collections Committee of the National Museum of American History. An information sheet is available from the Office of the Registrar, National Museum of American History.

PHOTODUPLICATION SERVICE
Available at prevailing rates, subject to rules and procedures of the Division and the Museum. Inquiries should be addressed to the Office of Printing and Photographic Services, National Museum of American History.

PUBLIC ACCESS
Exhibition galleries open from 10–5:30 daily except Christmas. Museum hours may be extended between Memorial Day and Labor Day. Research inquiries and information concerning objects not currently on exhibition write to the

Division of Physical Sciences
National Museum of American History
Smithsonian Institution
Washington, D.C. 20560

8R

Division of Political History

The Division of Political History is concerned with American history from before the Revolutionary War to the present as it is reflected in collections of objects associated with distinguished Americans as well as intellectual, political, and social movements. Holdings comprise three discrete collections: those which trace the development of American political campaigning, those which are associated with famous Americans, including the Presidents and the First Ladies, and those which illustrate American reform movements. While most of these 150,000 objects are American in origin and date from the 19th century to the present, there is also a choice selection of biographical material which dates from the 18th century.

The Division curates the largest and most comprehensive collection of American campaigning and inaugural materials extant. The Ralph E. Becker Collection and the DiSalle/Williams Collection are largely responsible for the

40,000 objects in this discrete group. Holdings date from 1789 to the present and include such forms as buttons, banners, badges, ribbons, jewelry, hats, smoking materials, lanterns, textile items, torches, toys and games.

The Division contains a wealth of decorative arts which are associated with historically important American places, events, and people—diplomats, explorers, inventors, military leaders, statesmen—and other notables. The associative collections include the well-known holdings of First Ladies gowns and small groups of miscellaneous costume items—canes, fans, gloves, jewelry, and umbrellas; White House ceramics; and Presidential costume materials ranging from business suits to complete sporting ensembles. The history of the White House itself is documented by upholstery and drapery samples which are supplemented by a model of the White House and information pertaining to its various renovations.

The Reform Collection encompasses objects associated with the temperance, anti-war, women's rights, civil rights, and voting rights movements. Holdings include banners, buttons, posters, pamphlets, costume materials, and a few pieces of furniture, some of which are associated with leaders of these movements.

CLASSIFIED CATALOG OF OBJECTS

Architectural Elements

small collection of interior architectural elements and fragments, hardware; base metals, marble, stained glass, and wood (from the White House and houses of other important Americans); early 19th through early 20th centuries.

Ceramics

550 porcelain tablewares used by the Presidents and their families both in the White House and in their private homes; China, England, France, USA; 18th through 20th centuries.

150 porcelain tablewares associated with famous Americans; various origins; 18th century to the present.

275 earthenware, stoneware, and porcelain campaign items including souvenirs, tablewares, and tiles; Europe, primarily USA; early 19th century through present day.

small collection of porcelain figures, snuff bottles, and tablewares; China, Europe; 18th and 19th centuries.

Costume (Garments and Accessories)

100 First Ladies gowns and 900 costume accessories (including gloves, purses, shawls, shoes); England, France, USA; late 18th century through present.

150 famous American men's and women's costumes and 1,850 accessories (including buttons, fans, gloves, hats, lace, parasols, shoes); primarily USA; late 18th century through present.

125 umbrellas and walking sticks; primarily USA; late 18th and 20th centuries.

50 campaign, parade, and patriotic costume items; USA; mid-19th century to present.

Furniture

275 pieces of furniture (including pieces from the U.S. Capitol Building); Asia, Europe, primarily England, USA; 18th century through present.

Glass

75 cut, enameled, engraved, and gilded glass tablewares used by the Presidents and their families both in the White House and in their private homes; Europe, USA; late 18th through 20th centuries.

100 glass tablewares which belonged to famous Americans; Europe, USA; late 18th through 20th centuries.

125 glass campaign bottles, flasks, paperweights, and tablewares; primarily USA; mid-19th century to present.

small collection of glass tablewares; Europe, USA; late 19th and early 20th centuries.

Heating and Lighting Devices

100 campaign and parade lanterns and torches (a unique and comprehensive collection); USA; mid-19th to early 20th centuries.

50 pieces of domestic fireplace equipment and lighting devices (including candlesticks, chandeliers, lamps, sconces, torchères); USA; 19th and 20th centuries.

Jewelry

150 pieces of jewelry (including associative, commemorative, costume, decorations, mourning, and presentation pieces); various origins, primarily USA; 18th century through present.

500 pieces of jewelry (including campaign, commemorative, and inaugural); primarily USA; 19th century to present.

Metalwork: Base Metals

small collection of brass, bronze, copper, iron boxes, figures, household utensils, and miscellaneous items; primarily USA; late 18th century to present.

Metalwork: Precious Metals

200 commemorative and presentation pieces; Belgium, China, England, France, Russia, South America, primarily USA; late 18th century to present.

flatware and hollow ware; Belgium, China, England, France, Russia, South America, USA; late 18th century to present.

Musical Instruments

small collection of keyboard, percussion, string, and wind instruments; primarily USA; early 19th through 20th centuries.

Textiles

50 fragments, samples, samplebooks and complete sets of curtains, draperies, and upholstery fabrics (including several used in the White House); primarily USA; 19th and early 20th centuries.

small collection of carpet, rugs, or other floor coverings; France, Middle East, USA; late 18th through 19th centuries.

small collection of associative or presentation bed coverings, decorative needleworked items, table linens; various origins, primarily USA; late 18th century to the present.

Timepieces and Measuring Devices
50 shelf clocks and watches; Europe, USA; late 18th to 19th centuries.
small collection of measuring devices; Europe, USA; late 18th to 19th centuries.

Toys and Games
75 board games, dolls, ivory chess sets, some campaign material; USA; late 18th century to present.
3 doll houses (2 with 785 miniature furnishings); USA; late 19th through mid-20th centuries.

FINDING AIDS
Card catalog arranged by donor.
Supplementary index arranged by associative name and object type. This file refers user back to the donor file.
Accession file and catalogue books arranged by number.
Photographic file by subject matter.

SELECTED PUBLICATIONS
Collins, Herbert R. *Political Campaign Torches*. Contributions from the Museum of History and Technology, no. 46. Washington, D.C.: Smithsonian Institution Press, 1966.
This catalog describes political campaign torches and related lighting devices which were used in street parades and rallies from 1837 to 1900. Photographs of thirty-two torches and patent designs are included.
———. *Threads of History: Americana Recorded on Cloth, 1775 to the Present*. Washington, D.C.: Smithsonian Institution Press, 1979.
This pictorial record of American history depicts the nation's cultural, political, and social past as it has appeared on bandannas and banners, quilts and samplers, pennants and broadsides, and other textiles. The more than 1,500 illustrated objects are primarily from the Division's collections.
Klapthor, Margaret Brown. *The First Ladies Hall*. Washington, D.C.: Smithsonian Institution Press, 1980.
This booklet is illustrated with photographs of the exhibition of dresses worn by First Ladies from the Washington administration to the present. Period room settings which display the dresses in the types of surroundings in which they were originally worn are included in the nine illustrations.
———. *Official White House China: 1789 to the Present*. Washington, D.C.: Smithsonian Institution Press, 1975.
This volume explores the written records of ceramics purchased with public funds for the residence of the president. Additionally, it is an attempt to reconcile both these records with surviving pieces and to identify pieces which have association with the President's House. This volume contains ninety-seven illustrations, many of which are of pieces in the Division's collection. Included in the appendix is a reprint of *The White House Porcelain Service: Designs by an American Artist, Illustrating Exclusively American Fauna*

and Flora. By Haviland and Company. New York, 1879.

————. *Presentation Pieces in the Museum of History and Technology.* Contributions from the Museum of History and Technology, no. 47. Washington, D.C.: Smithsonian Institution Press, 1966, pp. 81–108.

This is a descriptive and interpretative catalog of twenty-one pieces of presentation silver in the Museum's collections. Thirteen illustrated objects are in the Division of Political History's collection.

Klapthor, Margaret B.; Collins, Herbert R.; Mayo, Edith P.; and Sawyer, Peggy. *We the People: The American People and Their Government.* Washington, D.C.: Smithsonian Institution Press, 1975.

This volume records the growth of the United States government and its effect on Americans. Photographs of the "We the People" exhibition are included.

LENDING POLICY

Loans are granted to educational institutions for exhibition. Loans must be approved by the Curator and are subject to review by the Collections Committee of the National Museum of American History. An information sheet is available from the Office of the Registrar, National Museum of American History.

PHOTODUPLICATION SERVICE

Available at prevailing rates, subject to rules and procedures of the Division and the Museum. Inquiries should be addressed to the Office of Printing and Photographic Services, National Museum of American History.

PUBLIC ACCESS

Exhibition galleries open from 10–5:30 daily except Christmas. Museum hours may be extended between Memorial Day and Labor Day. Research inquiries and information concerning objects not currently on exhibition write to the

> Division of Political History
> National Museum of American History
> Smithsonian Institution
> Washington, D.C. 20560

8s

Division of Textiles

The Division of Textiles is concerned with fabrics as well as implements and machinery pertaining to the production and use of textiles in the United States and to the history of textile technology. The majority of the collection's approximately 45,000 objects reflect the development of the American Textile industry up to the twentieth century.

An extensive array of needlework and weaving techniques is represented in holdings of embroideries and laces, counterpanes and coverlets, quilts and other needleworked bedcovers, and of carpets and rugs. In addition, there are large collections of textile processing devices, patent models, and full-size sewing machines. Holdings, which are primarily American and western European, date from the 18th through the 20th centuries; the nineteenth century is best represented in this collection.

CLASSIFIED CATALOG OF OBJECTS

Basketry

125 baskets; Philippine Islands, USA; early 19th to early 20th centuries, primarily early 20th century.

Machinery and Tools

1,000 needlework accessories, kits, and tools (including clamps, frames, needles, and thimbles); Europe, USA; 18th through 20th centuries.

1,500 sewing machines and attachments (including full-size machines and models, some highly decorated); USA; mid-19th to 20th centuries.

150 spinning and weaving devices and textile processing implements; primarily USA; 19th century.

Textiles

175 coverlets and woven counterpanes, primarily handwoven; USA; late 18th through early 20th centuries.

350 quilts and needleworked bedcovers (including appliquéd, crocheted, embroidered, knitted, pieced, and other techniques); USA; mid-18th through early 20th centuries.

400 embroidered samplers, mourning and other pictures, costume and household accessories (techniques include candlewicking, canvas work, crewel, perforated cardboard, drawnwork, raised wool work, stumpwork, white-on-white); Europe, primarily USA; 17th through early 20th centuries.

2,000 laces and lacelike structures (techniques include bobbin, crocheting, drawnwork, embroidered net, knitting, knotting, macrame, netting, and tape lace); Belgium, France, Italy, USA; 17th through early 20th centuries.

100 woven shawls; Europe and Middle East, primarily Kashmir; 19th century.

200 hand and machine woven carpeting, carpet bags, and rugs (including full-scale items, manufacturer's samples, and patent models. Other examples of carpets and rugs are braided, crocheted, embroidered, hooked, knitted.); primarily USA; late 18th through 20th centuries.

150 Jacquard-woven silk pictures, many commemorative; China, Europe, USA; mid-19th through 20th centuries.

printed fabrics; primarily England, France, USA; 18th to 20th centuries.

woven silk and silk mixture fabrics (including brocades, damasks, velvets); England, France; 17th through 19th centuries, primarily 18th century.

silk and cotton fabrics collected by Commodore Matthew Perry; Japan; ca. 1856.

collection of samples of silk costume fabrics made by the Paragon Silk Co. of Paterson, New Jersey; late 19th century.

costume fabrics and trimmings from a Cleveland, Ohio, couturier shop; early 20th century.

examples of dyes and dyeing in dyers' manuals; primarily England, France, Germany, USA; 18th through 20th centuries.

costume fabrics; Europe; USA; 17th through 20th centuries.

narrow goods (bands, ribbons, and tapes); Europe, USA; 18th through 20th centuries.

FINDING AIDS

Card catalog arranged by catalog number.

Indexes of photographs and artifacts arranged by subject.

Books of photographs and color slides are arranged by subject.

SELECTED PUBLICATIONS

Cooper, Grace Rogers. *The Copp Family Textiles*. Smithsonian Studies in History and Technology, no. 7. Washington, D.C.: Smithsonian Institution Press, 1971.

This catalog includes historical and technical information pertaining to a collection of late 18th and early 19th century household fabrics which belonged to a family that lived in Stonington, Connecticut. There are fifty-eight illustrations of items in the collection.

———. *The Sewing Machine: Its Invention and Development*. Washington, D.C.: Smithsonian Institution Press, 1976. (This book was originally published under the title *The Invention of the Sewing Machine*, 1967.)

This well-illustrated volume describes the evolution of the sewing machine from the 19th century. Illustrations of more than 200 advertisements, machines, and accessories.

LENDING POLICY

Loans are granted to educational institutions for exhibition. Loans must be approved by the Curator and are subject to review by the Collections Committee of the National Museum of American History. An information sheet is available from the Office of the Registrar, National Museum of American History.

PHOTODUPLICATION SERVICE

Available at prevailing rates, subject to rules and procedures of the Division and the Museum. Inquiries should be addressed to the Office of Printing and Photographic Services, National Museum of American History.

PUBLIC ACCESS

Exhibition galleries open from 10–5:30 daily except Christmas. Museum hours may be extended between Memorial Day and Labor Day. Research inquiries and

information concerning objects not currently on exhibition write to the

Division of Textiles
National Museum of American History
Smithsonian Institution
Washington, D.C. 20560

8T

Division of Transportation

The Division of Transportation is concerned with the history of American maritime, railroad, and road transportation from the eighteenth century to the present. In addition to both full-size and model vehicles, there are associated accessories.

Holdings of animal and motor powered vehicles contain a few elaborately painted carriages and several pieces of horse gear, notably bridle rosettes. The maritime collection includes examples of needleworked and macrame items made by American sailors. The rail collection includes an inlaid panel from a late 19th century pullman car, as well as several locomotives and a street car, which are decoratively painted.

CLASSIFIED CATALOG OF OBJECTS

Architectural Elements
skylight and plaster reliefs from the S.S. *Majestic* and interior panels from the
    S.S. *United States*; England, USA, respectively; ca. 1889 and 1952, respectively.

Ceramics
tableware from the S.S. *United States* and from railroad dining cars (including
    pieces by Mayer China Co., Buffalo China Co., and Onondaga Pottery Co.);
    USA; 1925–52.
model of a stoneware merchant's wagon; unidentified origin; probably 19th century.

Costume (Garments and Accessories)
small collection of rail conductor's uniforms; USA; mid-19th to 20th centuries.

Furniture
railroad station bench; USA; ca. 1890.
side chair from the riverboat S.S. *J.M. White II*; France; ca. 1878.
small collection of furniture from the S.S. *United States*; USA; ca. 1952.

Glass
tableware from the S.S. *United States*; USA; ca. 1952.

Metalwork: Precious Metals
presentation belt mounted with five silver medallions; Scotland; 1880
silver watch fob in the form of a train; USA; ca. 1890.
enamel-decorated gold box given to Joseph Francis by Napoleon III; France; 1856.
silver and silver-plated flatware from the S.S. *J.M. White II* and the S.S. *United States* (including pieces by Gorham Manufacturing Co., Lamberton Sterling, International Silver Co., R. Wallace); USA; ca. 1878 and 1952, respectively.
silver W. K. Vanderbilt cup made by Tiffany and Co.; New York; 1905.
silver boatswain's trumpet made by Samuel Lewis and presented by President James Buchanan; Washington, D.C.; 1858.
silver presentation model of a World War I merchant ship; USA; ca. 1918.

Other Materials
small collection of leather fire buckets; USA; late 18th century.

Timepieces and Measuring Devices
watch by Joseph Johnson for the Camden and Amboy Railroad; Liverpool, England; ca. 1850.

FINDING AIDS
Indexes arranged by subject.

SELECTED PUBLICATIONS
Post, Robert C. *American Maritime Enterprise: Checklist, Guide, Acknowledgments.* Washington, D.C.: National Museum of History and Technology, 1978. Checklist of the permanent exhibition "American Maritime Enterprise" in the National Museum of American History.

LENDING POLICY
Loans are granted to educational institutions for exhibition. Loans must be approved by the Curator and are subject to review by the Collections Committee of the National Museum of American History. An information sheet is available from the Office of the Registrar, National Museum of American History.

PHOTODUPLICATION SERVICE
Available at prevailing rates, subject to rules and procedures of the Division and the Museum. Inquiries should be addressed to the Office of Printing and Photographic Services, National Museum of American History.

PUBLIC ACCESS
Exhibition galleries open from 10–5:30 daily except Christmas. Museum hours may be extended between Memorial Day and Labor Day. Research inquiries and information concerning objects not currently on exhibition write to the

Division of Transportation
National Museum of American History
Smithsonian Institution
Washington, D.C. 20560

8U

National Numismatics Collection

The National Numismatics Collections are concerned with the entire spectrum of materials which illustrate the historical development of money and medals. Characteristic examples of coins, decorations, documents of value (including bills of exchange, bonds, checks, paper currencies, scrip, and stock certificates), medals, and tokens from the crossroads of history document political, military, and social events throughout the world. Collections also trace the manufacturing process of coins and medals from the artist's concept to the creation of the model, to the preparation of the dies, and finally to the striking. Scholars studying the history of both design and early American silversmiths and engravers, Ephraim Brasher and Christian Gobrecht, to name two, will find these collections of interest.

Medallic holdings include Indian Peace medals which date from the late eighteenth century until 1889, commemorative and art medals, Smithsonian Award medals, and a large group of medals commemorating George Washington.

FINDING AIDS
Card catalog arranged by donor.

SELECTED PUBLICATIONS
Clain-Stefanelli, Elvira E. *Highlights from the Money Collection of the Chase Manhattan Bank.* Washington, D.C.: National Museum of History and Technology, 1979.

This generously illustrated booklet describes the exhibition of the Chase Manhattan Bank Collection of coinage and paper money, as well as primitive media of exchange.

Clain-Stefanelli, Elvira E., and Clain-Stefanelli, Vladimir. *The Beauty and Lore of Coins, Currency, and Medals.* Croton-on-Hudson, New York: Riverwood Publishers, 1975.

This volume is profusely illustrated with pieces from the collection. It documents the history of coins, medals, and currency from ancient times to the present day.

———. *Medals Commemorating Battles of the American Revolution.* Washington, D.C.: National Museum of History and Technology, 1973.

This illustrated booklet documents the design and historical background of the earliest official medals of the United States.

———. *Monnaies europeennes et monnaies coloniales americaines entre 1450 et 1789.* Fribourg, Switzerland: Office de Livre, 1978. (In French).

This volume presents the development of European and American coinage from the artistic, economic, and historical points of view from 1450 to 1789.

LENDING POLICY
Loans are granted to educational institutions for exhibition. Loans must be approved by the Curator and are subject to review by the Collections Committee of the National Museum of American History. An information sheet is available from the Office of the Registrar, National Museum of American History.

PHOTODUPLICATION SERVICE
Available at prevailing rates, subject to rules and procedures of the Division and the Museum. Inquiries should be addressed to the Office of Printing and Photographic Services, National Museum of American History.

PUBLIC ACCESS
Exhibition galleries open from 10–5:30 daily except Christmas. Museum hours may be extended between Memorial Day and Labor Day. Research inquiries and information concerning objects not currently on exhibition write to the

National Numismatics Collection
National Museum of American History
Smithsonian Institution
Washington, D.C. 20560

9

National Museum of Natural History And National Museum of Man

The purposes of the National Museum of Natural History and the National Museum of Man are fourfold: to obtain, preserve, and maintain collections representing both the natural and cultural history of our planet, and when possible, our universe; to study and interpret this history through the use of these collections; to make these collections available for study to scholars; and to share the evidence represented by its collections and other studies with both the scientific and general public.

28 Vessel, collected in 1885.
    Zuni, New Mexico.
    Painted earthenware.

29 Brazier (*hibachi*), collected in 1882.
Japan.
Lacquer with raised gold lacquer.

The collections of the National Museum of Natural History, numbering approximately sixty-three million specimens and assembled over more than a century, rank among the most important research resources in the world. In many areas, the collections are unequaled. As a result, the Museum is one of the major world centers of basic systematic (taxonomic) research in the natural sciences including the nature, relationships, origin, and evolution of plants, animals, man and his cultures; the origin, formation, and structure of the earth and its extraterrestrial neighbors.

The granite-faced classical style building was designed by Hornblower and

Marshall of Washington, D.C. Construction of the central portion began in 1904 and was completed in 1911.

9 A

Department of Anthropology

The Department of Anthropology is concerned with the study of man as a cultural and biological species from the time of his earliest existence to the present. Systematic holdings of over 1¾ million specimens include archeological, ethnological, and physical anthropological materials relating primarily to non-European and non-Euroamerican peoples. These encyclopedic collections contain human artifacts and material remains which are the tangible representation of individual cultures. The National Anthropological Archives is also part of the Department of Anthropology. The Archives contains anthropologists' and researchers' diaries, documents, letters, maps, notes, and photographs which document the people, places, and things relating to anthropology.

Archeological collections in the Department of Anthropology contain materials excavated from the earth. These artifactual and ecofactual specimens represent the cultures of the past, most of which no longer exist. The archeological collection is arranged geographically by country, state, and site. Within this geographical framework, artifacts of like materials are stored together, for example—groups of ceramic sherds, stone points, and textile fragments. Holdings relate primarily to Native American peoples with a few Old World pieces.

The Department's ethnological holdings were collected from, and therefore represent, the material culture of historic, non-Western peoples. The collection contains a wide range of objects—everyday and outstanding, new and used, complete and unfinished, archaic and modern—all of which contribute to a complete understanding of a people and their culture.

These large and diverse holdings are studied and stored according to cultural areas, which often transcend and supercede political delineations. Artifacts are stored by function, material, and size within each culture's storage area.

The anthropological system of arranging artifacts initially by culture and secondarily by function, material, and size requires researchers to have a basic understanding of the cultures of the world—what materials they used, what types of objects they made, and how those objects were used.

Ethnologists first began to collect cohesive groups of artifacts in the early nineteenth century. Some of the artifacts gathered during early expeditions may in fact predate the mid-19th century. However, without a recorded provenience (origin) the precise date of production may not be known. Moreover, researchers should note that the date the object was collected may not have any relation to the date when it was made.

Information concerning provenience is generally noted according to the name of the region at the time of collection. Hence, researchers must know to check, for example: Abyssinia as well as Ethiopia, Congo as well as Zaire, Siam as well as Thailand, Persia as well as Iran, Dakota Territory as well as North and South Dakota.

The National Anthropological Archives was organized in 1965 as a part of the Department of Anthropology. It is the successor to the archives of the former Bureau of American Ethnology. The purpose of the Archives is both to serve as a depository of the records of the Department and its predecessor organizations, and to collect private papers relating to the cultures of the world and the history of anthropology.

Because the Bureau of American Ethnology was primarily interested in the North American Indians, the Archives' collection of manuscripts, official records, and photographs dating between 1847 and 1970, is among the world's finest resources for the study of Native Americans. The Archives continues to have a special interest in American Indians in addition to its broader, and more worldwide, interests. For additional information see the *Finders' Guide to Prints and Drawings in the Smithsonian Institution*, by Lynda C. Claassen.

9_{A1}

African Ethnology Collection

The African collection comprises approximately 6,000 objects dating from the mid-19th century through the present, with strongest holdings from the Congo Basin (Zaire), West African and North African regions. Forms which are best represented include basketry, costume items, musical instruments, and weaponry.

CONGO BASIN COLLECTION
There are more than 2,000 objects from the Cameroon, the Congo (Zaire), and Gabon. Included in these holdings is the Herbert Ward Collection which was assembled with the help of Sir Henry M. Stanley in the late 1890s. It is interesting to note that Ward used these materials to decorate his sculpture studio. Carved wooden forms in the collection include bowls, figures, masks, spoons, and stools. Fiber and textile items are represented by bark cloth, grass, and raffia costume and domestic items, as well as examples of the finely woven pile cloth called Kasai cloth. Personal ornaments are of beads, bone, copper, feathers, iron, ivory, and seeds. The metalworking tradition of the Congo Basin area is illustrated by manillas (once used as a means of exchange), figures, and knives.

WEST AFRICAN COLLECTION
The West African collection comprises more than 1,100 objects from Dahomey (Benin), the Gold Coast (Ghana), the Ivory Coast, Liberia, Mali, Nigeria, Sene-

gal, Togo, and Upper Volta. Metalwork, for which this area is well known, is represented by Benin bronzes (from Nigeria), and Ashanti gold weights, as well as brass and iron figures, personal ornaments, and vessels from other West African cultures.

West African textiles and costume holdings comprise cotton textile samples, blankets, and raffia costumes, along with looms, weaving tools, and tie-dyeing samples.

Containers are of basketry, unglazed earthenware, carved and incised gourds, and skin.

Carved wooden forms in the West African collection include figures, headpieces, masks, musical instruments, shields, spoons, and stools.

NORTH AFRICAN COLLECTION

The North African collection is made up of more than 900 objects from Algeria, Egypt, Libya, Morocco, and Tunisia. Ceramic items include glazed (blue, green, white, yellow, and copper lusters) and unglazed earthenware figures, lamps, and vessels. There are also similar items of pierced or otherwise decorated brass, copper, and tin.

Metalworking is illustrated in holdings of jewelry, religious objects, and weaponry, in addition to those forms listed above. There are bracelets, earrings, necklaces, and reliquaries of brass, enamel, and silver. Similarly, firearms, edged weapons, and powder horns are decorated with cast and engraved brass and silver mounts.

The North African leatherworking tradition is represented by embossed, painted, and woven items—bags, bottles, cushions, horsegear, and shoes.

Costume holdings comprise men's, women's, and children's wear, some decorated with embroidery and applied mirrors. Textile processes are documented by embroidery and weaving samples, as well as blankets, rugs, and costume fabrics.

The North African basketry collection includes fans, sieves, and containers of all sizes.

EAST CENTRAL AFRICAN COLLECTION

The East Central African collection includes more than 800 objects from Kenya, Rwanda, southern Sudan, Tanzania (formerly Tanganyika and Zanzibar), Uganda, and northern Zambia. Although holdings include materials from many groups, the Hutu, Masai, and Tutsi are best represented. The woodcarving tradition of East Central Africa is illustrated by numerous bottles, figures, headrests, ladles, masks, and stools. Weaponry (bows, arrows, and spears), painted shields, and ceremonial materials are also included in this collection.

Costume holdings from this area of Africa comprise beaded skirts and ornaments, some of which are made of feathers. Beads are also used to decorate some of the finely woven basketry container in the collection. There are also containers made of carved and incised gourds, basketry, and carved wood. Musical instruments and bark cloth are additionally contained in these holdings.

SOUTHERN AFRICA COLLECTION
There are more than 600 objects from the countries of Southern Africa—Angola, Madagascar, the Republic of South Africa, Zambia, and Zimbabwe. These holdings include bark cloth (some decorated with geometric patterns), basketry items (finely woven containers, some made with dyed fibers), costume items and beaded ornaments, earthenware vessels, musical instruments, weaponry, and carved wooden forms (bowls, headdresses, headrests, masks, and pipes).

NILE RIVER VALLEY AND EASTERN HORN COLLECTION
The Nile River Valley and Eastern Horn collection comprises Egyptian, Ethiopian, and Sudanese materials (approximately 500 objects) from several diverse groups. Holdings from the Amharic, Islamic, and Judaic cultures are closely related and similar to the items in the North African collection.

Tribal material from the Nile River Valley-Eastern Horn area, however, relates more closely to the material cultures of Sub-Saharan Africa than to objects made by members of the Mediterranean-area groups. There are basketry containers, beaded and woven grass costume items, earthenware dishes (some with carved and/or stamped designs), carved wooden headrests, musical instruments, shell ornaments, parade shields (some decorated with engraved brass ornaments), and weapons.

9_{A2}

Asian Ethnology Collection

The Asian Collection comprises approximately 30,000 objects. Holdings are most numerous from Japan and Korea, followed by those from China and Taiwan, the Indian Subcontinent, Southeast Asia, the eastern Mediterranean.

JAPANESE AND KOREAN COLLECTION
The Japanese and Korean collection (total of 10,000 objects) comprises materials dating from the mid-19th to the early 20th century, including numerous objects collected by Matthew C. Perry during his expedition in Japan, 1852–54. The entire collection is rich in holdings of various forms (costume items, domestic furnishings, weaponry, and tools) and materials (bronze, ceramics, and silk).

The comprehensive collection of ceramic items comprises Japanese and Korean earthenware, stoneware, and porcelain forms dating from the 14th to the mid-20th centuries. These holdings are primarily teawares and figures, however writing equipment, large vessels, and large figures are also represented. Additionally, there is a unique series of porcelain-making materials, circa 1885, including bodies, glazes, and examples of the stages of porcelain production.

The Japanese and Korean collection contains an uncommon group of tools, materials, and examples of a variety of items in progressive stages of production. The techniques of carving ivory, lacquer, and wood are all illustrated by carving tools and unfinished examples. Metalworking and enameling are likewise documented by pieces in progress.

Complementing these examples of items in various stages of production, there are large holdings of completed works, many of which date from mid-to late-19th century Japan and Korea. Bamboo, ivory, tortoiseshell, and stone items include boxes, figures of all sizes, *netsuke*, ornamental pieces, religious shrines, and writing equipment. The collection also includes a variety of lacquer ware items—boxes, *inrō*, miniature and full-size furniture and teawares—many of which are decorated with inlay and applied surface decorations. Carved wooden objects include figures, *netsuke*, panels, and screens. Holdings of metalwork, some of which are decorated with enameling, are made of brass, bronze, and cloisonné enamel; forms represented are candlesticks, matchsafes, mirrors, teawares, and small decorative objects.

Japanese and Korean furniture and furnishings constitute yet another sizable group of objects. Representative forms include: boxes, chests, screens, shelves (set with inlay, lacquer, porcelain, and painted silk panels), and lighting devices of ceramic, metal, textiles, and wood.

There are large holdings of Japanese and Korean costume items and accessories, as well as textile examples. Men's, women's, and children's wear ranges from everyday cotton items to silk bridal and court dresses. Many of these silk items are embroidered with silk and/or metallic thread. Costume accessories are also well represented by such forms as hats, ceremonial headdresses, umbrellas, flat and folding fans, and shoes. Finally, there is a small collection of embroidered items made by Japanese schoolgirls.

Japanese dress is also represented by costume dolls. There are several fully armored Samurai dolls; cloth, paper, and textile dolls; and Korean doll-like puppets. Miniature furniture and a doll house are also included in these holdings. Other leisure-time materials comprise kites, smoking equipment and accessories, musical instruments, and miniature and full-size masks.

There is a comprehensive collection of Japanese and Korean weaponry along with Samurai armor. Japanese material, some of which dates from the 16th century, comprises complete suits of armor (some gilded and lacquered) *menuke*, sword ensembles, sword stands, *tsuba*, and highly decorated saddles (tooled leather and lacquer stirrups).

MAINLAND CHINA AND TAIWAN

The Chinese collection (total of 6,000 objects) dates primarily from the late 19th and early 20th centuries. As with the Japanese collection, holdings comprise a variety of materials and forms.

The large holdings of Chinese ceramics include earthenware, stoneware, and porcelain objects decorated with a variety of glazes. Although teawares are most numerous, there are many figures, tiles, and vases included in this collection. Chinese export wares made for western markets are also represented.

Stoneware and porcelain are only two of many materials found in the snuff bottle collection. There are bottles of carved crystal, glass, ivory, jade, lacquer, and stone. A few date from the 18th century, however, the majority are from the 19th century.

There are sizable holdings of Chinese furniture and furnishings. Furniture forms include screens, tables, shelves, compartmented chests, and chairs, some of which are set with porcelain, painted glass, carved ivory, jade, lacquer, and mother-of-pearl panels. Heating and lighting devices (primarily braziers, candlesticks, and lanterns) are made of brass, bronze, and earthenware. Other small domestic items—boxes, figures, and vessels—are of brass, bronze, enamel, pewter, and silver. Religious and decorative objects (boxes, chess sets, containers, and figures) are of carved coconuts, cased glass, ivory, jade, lacquer ware, stone, and wood.

Holdings of Chinese toys and amusements comprise paper kites, which were exhibited in the 1876 Centennial Exposition, musical instruments, smoking equipment, and costume dolls.

There is a sizable collection of Chinese costume and textile items. Costume material ranges from grass hats to bridal headdresses, embroidered scarves, imperial robes, and shoes (of grass, leather, and embroidered silk) for bound feet. Accessories comprise flat and folding fans of ivory, lacquer, and wood, some of which are contained in fitted boxes. Jewelry and personal adornments are again varied (bracelets, buckles, charms, earrings, hair ornaments, nail guards, and rings) and are of numerous materials (crystal, enamel, gold, jade, seeds, embroidered silk, silver, and wood). Textile holdings date from the 18th century and include lengths of fabric, as well as embroidered silk wall hangings, pillow covers, and other panels.

The collection contains Chinese hand tools used for agriculture, iron working, rugmaking, and woodworking. There are several models of tools along with carved wooden scenes of everyday activities.

The collection includes a small number of objects from the traditional cultures of Taiwan, specifically, from the Paiwan and Yami groups. Carved wooden items are most numerous and notable particularly wedding cups, figures, shields, and architectural elements. Basketry containers and hats are also well represented. The several costume items include embroidered textile, jewelry, combs, and headdresses.

INDIAN SUBCONTINENT COLLECTION

The Asian collection comprises large holdings from the Indian Subcontinent (total of 7,000 objects). While over half of these objects are from India and West Pakistan, there is material (in order of decreasing quantity) from Afghanistan, Andaman and Nicobar islands, Assam, East Pakistan (Bangladesh), Bhutan, Nepal, Sri Lanka (Ceylon), and Tibet. The majority of these objects were collected between the late 19th and mid-20th centuries.

Holdings include basketry of all sizes and types, for example, fish traps, agricultural implements, trays, and hats. Basketmaking techniques are illustrated by examples in various stages of completion.

There is a large collection of woven textile items including cotton, silk, and wool costume fabrics. Yarns, looms, and weaving accessories illustrate the materials and processes used to weave these textiles. Similarly, dyes, carved wooden printing blocks, stencils, and sample books illustrate the various processes and techniques used to decorate these weavings.

The collection contains large and varied holdings of men's, women's, and children's costume items from silk saris, to Kashmir shawls, to sheepskin mountaineer's coats. Many of these articles are richly embroidered; some are decorated with beads, mirrors, and sequins. Accessories also vary from silk turbans to heavy knee-high boots. Additional forms include flat and folding fans; headdresses decorated with feathers, gold foil paper, and small mirrors; and headdresses of carved bone and pith. Jewelry forms—belts, bracelets, chatelaines, earrings, necklaces, and rings—are of many materials includings beads, brass, coral, enamel, glass, gold, ivory, jade, shell, silver, and turquoise.

Metalwork is represented by groups of edged weapons and armor, heating and lighting equipment (braziers, candlesticks, firestands, and tinderboxes), and a variety of containers (boxes, bowls, and tewares). Some of these metal objects are decorated with contrasting metal inlay.

Vessels and religious figures are made of both glazed and unglazed earthenware. Other religious items include—painted alabaster, bronze, carved, gilded and/or painted wood figures; bronze ceremonial daggers; brass and copper prayer wheels; embroidered altar linens; polychrome wood masks; and highly decorated musical instruments (bells, gongs, horns, sitars). Additionally, there are several pieces of ornamented ceremonial horsegear of worked leather, and silver with tassel decorations.

Holdings of domestic items comprise a few carved wooden architectural elements, several chairs, polychrome bed frames, and a number of toys and games (including a miniature gaming table and chess sets of carved ivory).

There is a large and important group of materials and tools which illustrate processes and finished products. This material was acquired in West Pakistan and Sri Lanka during the mid-1960s. Metalworking traditions are represented by examples of brass casting and inlay, blacksmithing, coppersmithing, metalengraving, silversmithing, wiredrawing, and gold and silver foil production. Textile and textile related processes include dyeing, felting, printing, and weaving. Brickmaking and potter's tools, equipment, and raw materials document the manufacture of these ceramic items. Additionally, there are implements to carve bone, crystal, horn, ivory, marble, onyx, shell, stone, and wood. The leatherworking craft is represented by tools for embossing, saddlemaking, shoemaking, and tanning. There are also examples illustrating the lacquering process.

SOUTHEAST ASIAN COLLECTION
The Southeast Asian collection comprises material (4,700 objects) from Burma, Cambodia, Laos, Malaya, Thailand, and Viet Nam. Holdings date from the mid-19th to the mid-20th century and are particularly strong in Siamese and Burmese objects.

Entertainment materials are numerous in this collection. There are drums, gongs, string and wind instruments, as well as shadow puppets, marionettes, and cutout figures. Kites and small ceramic figures are also included in the holdings.

Ceremonial and religious objects include highly decorated presentation swords, as well as polychrome masks and Buddhist figures made of bronze, stone, and wood. There are temple furnishings, small elaborately decorated household shrines, and richly embroidered ceremonial robes.

In the large costume collection, several of the cotton and silk items date from the late 1850s; however, most date from the late 19th and early 20th centuries. Several are decorated with embroidery, shells, and silver ornaments. Accessories include brushes, combs, fans, jewelry, shoes, and other forms.

As with the other Asian collections, boxes, teawares, and other containers are of a variety of materials—basketry, brass, earthenware, enamel, lacquer ware, porcelain, silver, stoneware, and wood.

The Southeast Asian collection contains a variety of objects which were given to the 1876 Centennial Exposition by the King of Siam. Material ranges from costume items to embroidered pillow covers, boat models (including one of the Royal Barge), and machine and tool models.

EASTERN MEDITERRANEAN COLLECTION

The Eastern Mediterranean is represented by holdings (2,000 objects) from Arabia, Armenia, Iran, Iraq, Lebanon, Palestine, Syria, and Turkey. Most of this material was collected during the late 19th and early 20th centuries.

Costume holdings comprise men's, women's, and children's items from silk fez to wooden shoes inlaid with ivory and mother-of-pearl. There are silk, cotton, and wool textile samples as well as some embroidered items, table linens, wall hangings, saddle blankets, and shawls. Rugs are complemented by rug-making equipment, patterns, printing blocks, and dye samples.

Other craft processes represented in the collection include metalwork (goldsmithing, silversmithing, and wiredrawing), leatherworking (embossing and saddlemaking), ceramic productions (glazed and unglazed tiles and vessels), as well as carpentry, inlay, glassmaking, and stone carving.

Ceramic items in the collection include earthenware, stoneware, and porcelain—lamps, decorative objects, tiles, and vessels, many of which were made for the 1876 Centennial Exposition.

The Eastern Mediterranean metalworking tradition is illustrated by several types of objects. There are firearms and edged weapons decorated with brass, enamel, and silver; silver jewelry and coffee services; brass candlesticks and chandeliers, and smoking pipes. Judaica (including *rimmonim, mezuzah,* scent sprinklers, and spice boxes) and eastern Orthodox objects (a crozier and a pair of elaborate finials) are also contained in this collection.

9A3

Middle American and
Caribbean Island Ethnology Collection

The Middle American and Carribean Island collection (totaling more than 5,000 objects) is strongest in materials from Guatemala and Mexico, Costa Rica and Panama. Holdings date primarily from the late 19th century to the present.

MEXICAN AND GUATEMALAN COLLECTION
The Mexican and Guatamelan collection (approximately 3,000 objects) encompasses materials from the Maya, Huichol, Seri, Tarahumara, Tarascan, Yaqui, and other indigenous groups, along with items from Catholicized village groups. This collection is particularly strong in textiles and costume items. There are several blankets, carrying cloths, and textile samples, along with a loom and weaving implements. Costume holdings comprise shawls, shirts, and trousers, many with brightly colored woven and/or embroidered designs. Personal ornaments of beads and coral, as well as woven grass fans, hats, and shoes are also included in this collection.

The collection's Mexican and Guatemalan containers and vessels are made of various materials—basketry, earthenware, glass, gourds (some carved, lacquered, or painted), and wood. Other forms made of these materials include toys, masks, and musical instruments.

COSTA RICAN AND PANAMANIAN COLLECTION
Costa Rican and Panamanian holdings (approximately 1,000 objects) are particularly strong in material from the Cuna of San Blas. This group, and others living in both the rain forest area and higher elevations, are represented by holdings of painted bark cloth, beaded costume items, and body ornaments (primarily necklaces made of bone, feathers, seeds, shell, and teeth). Holdings also include containers and vessels of basketry and earthenware, along with wooden drums, masks, stools, and a complete religious shrine.

A number of Panamanian *molas* are included in the collection. These reverse appliquéd patchwork panels were originally integrated into costume items, but are currently made solely as export goods.

CARIBBEAN COLLECTION
The Caribbean collection (approximately 1,000 objects) comprises items from the Bahamas, Barbados, Bermuda, Cuba, the Dominican Republic, Haiti, Jamaica, Puerto Rico, Trinidad, and the Virgin Islands. Largest holdings are from the Dominican Republic and Haiti. Vessels and containers in the collection are of various materials—basketry, earthenware, gourds, and wood. Other Caribbean materials include musical instruments (primarily stringed), carved and painted

wooden dolls, bark cloth, and embroidered textile costume items. The collection also comprises a unique group of Haitian voodoo altar materials.

9_{A4}

North American Ethnology Collection

The North American Ethnology collection in the Department of Anthropology is one of the most important and comprehensive collections of Native American material in the world (more than 46,000 objects). Many of the holdings were collected under the direction of the Bureau of American Ethnology, which was founded in 1879. The present holdings of the Department reflect both the history of American anthropology and the material culture of Native Americans. Holdings comprise not only common, everyday tools and implements, but also superlative examples of native art and workmanship. All of these objects were used by American Indians and, although the majority were also made by Native Americans, European and American trade goods (such as beads) are fully represented. Artifacts from the Southwest are most numerous, followed in order of descending number of objects, by those from the Arctic-Alaska region, Plains-Prairie, Northwest Coast, Northern California-Oregon-Washington, Great Basin, Great Lakes-Eastern Woodlands, Southeastern, Eastern Subarctic, and Northwestern Subarctic regions.

SOUTHWESTERN COLLECTION
The Southwestern collection (approximately 23,000 objects) is well known for its comprehensive holdings of pottery, basketry, textiles, and jewelry. There are more than 19,000 painted vessels and figures from the pueblos of Acoma, Hopi, Sia, and Zuni. Most were made and collected between 1870 and 1890. Also well-represented are southwestern basketry forms (primarily coiled); loom-woven blankets and costume items; silver and turquoise jewelry; and Hopi kachina dolls. Pueblos from which there are especially large holdings include Acoma, Hopi, Santa Clara, Sia, and Zuni, while non-pueblo groups include the Apache, Navaho, Pima, and Mohave.

ARCTIC-ALASKA COLLECTION
The comprehensive collection from the Arctic-Alaska region (approximately 8,000 objects) includes large holdings of Eskimo and Aleutian artifacts of worked bone, ivory, stone, and wood, many of which show Asian influence. There are carved and incised bone buttons, figures, and needlecases; skin boat models and costume items; carved, incised, and painted wood boxes, combs, dishes, figures, masks, and toggles; and dolls and hunting and fishing implements of all three materials. The collection also contains basketry and earthenware lamps.

30 Effigy birds, collected in 1888.
Zuni, New Mexico.
Painted earthenware.

PLAINS-PRAIRIE COLLECTION

The Plains-Prairie collection (approximately 5,800 objects) includes hundreds of bags, blankets, costume items and ornaments of beaded, feather worked, painted, or quilled skins. (It is interesting to note that porcupine quill embroidery is unique to the North American Indians.) Holdings of Arapaho, Cheyenne, and Sioux moccasins are particularly extensive. There is also a unique group of Kiowa painted tipi and shield models which were made for James Mooney of the Bureau of American Ethnology during his field studies of Indian history and art in southwestern Oklahoma, 1891–1904. Carved stone pipe bowls and decorated pipe stems form yet another distinguished group of Sioux artifacts.

NORTHWEST COAST COLLECTION

The Northwest Coast collection (approximately 3,000 objects) contains artifacts from the Bella Bella, Haida, Makah, and Tlingit cultures, among others. Forms include bone needlecases, horn spoons, basketry containers, and woven birch bark mats. There are also sizable holdings of boxes, canes, combs, dishes, masks, totem poles, and rattles of wood and/or slate (argillite), some of which are incised, inlaid, or painted.

NORTHERN CALIFORNIA-OREGON-WASHINGTON COLLECTION

The Northern California-Oregon-Washington holdings (approximately 2,000 artifacts) are best known for the exceptional basketry of the Hupa, Karok, and

Pomo. The collection comprises examples of superb coiled and twined baskets decorated with feather embroidery, shells, or beads. From southern California Indian groups there are also holdings of very fine baskets.

GREAT BASIN COLLECTION
The Great Basin collection (of 1,500 objects) is best represented by basketry and skin costume items, some of which are decorated with quill and beadwork. Collections of Paiute, Shoshone, and Ute materials are most numerous.

GREAT LAKES-EASTERN WOODLANDS COLLECTION
Holdings from the Great Lakes-Eastern Woodlands (approximately 1,200 objects) include many Chippewa and Iroquois artifacts, among other groups. There are numerous skin and textile costumes and bags decorated with ribbon, bead, and quillwork. Basketry, silver and German silver jewelry, and masks are all included in this collection.

SOUTHEASTERN COLLECTION
The Southeastern collection (approximately 1,000 objects) includes material from the Catawba and Chitimacha, primarily basketry and earthenware, and the Cherokee, primarily masks, and the Seminole. Seminole material is particularly strong in late 19th and early 20th century textiles, costume items, and costumed dolls. There are also representative holdings of machine-sewn decorative patchwork and applied work.

EASTERN SUBARTIC
From the Eastern Subarctic region, holdings (approximately 500 objects) are largest from the Cree, Montagnais, and Naskapi cultures, among others. This collection comprises worked skin costume items, many of which are beaded (primarily using glass trade beads but occasionally ornamented with bone, shell, or stone beads), painted, or quilled.

NORTHWESTERN SUBARCTIC COLLECTION
From the Northwestern Subarctic region there are approximately 400 objects including Athabascan (Northern) beaded and quillworked bags, along with personal ornaments.

9 A5

Pacific Ethnology Collection

The Pacific collection (also called the Oceanic collection) comprises approximately 21,000 ethnographic objects from Indonesia, Melanesia, Polynesia, Micronesia, Australia, and New Zealand. The most important collection is that assembled during the U. S. South Seas Exploring Expedition, led by Commodore Charles Wilkes from 1839 to 1843. This was the last exploratory expedition to depend on sailing vessels. Appropriately, this voyage inspired the writing of both *Moby Dick* and *Two Years Before the Mast*. Wilkes collected throughout the Pacific and added more than 2,000 objects to the collection.

The Department's Oceanic materials are varied in form, containing architectural elements, basketry items, body ornaments, costume items, and weaponry from all areas. The majority of objects are made of grass, wood, or other native cellulose materials. The primary subject of Pacific woodworking is the human form. Anthropomorphic images appear in the collection as burned, carved, incised, inlayed, and painted elements—in portions of ceremonial houses, bark paintings, canoe prows and paddles, shields and weaponry, and utilitarian objects. Many of these items were made for ceremonial or religious use.

Basketry, woven textiles, and tapa cloth (also called bark cloth) are well represented in the Oceanic collection. Basketry forms include bags, bowls, and fish traps, as well as body ornaments, fans, hats, and other costume items. Coarsely woven mats and matting used as both floor and wall coverings are included in these holdings.

The Pacific collection contains a large number of personal ornaments from all cultural areas. These holdings comprise everything from combs and headdresses, to belts and anklets. Various materials, primarily beads, feathers, shells, and teeth, are used as embellishments for these basketry, tapa, or textile bands.

31 Woman's jacket, collected in 1918–19.
Celebes Islands.
Painted bark cloth.

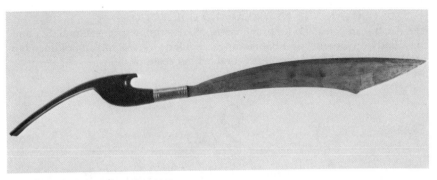

32 Sword (*pira*), collected in 1912.
Moro, Philippine Islands.
Metal and horn.

INDONESIAN COLLECTION

The Indonesian collection (approximately 11,000 objects) is strongest in materials from Borneo and the Philippines. Loom-woven textile holdings are most numerous, many of which are decorated with beads, embroidery, and paint. Additionally, there are large collections of early 20th century batiks, woven bags, baskets, mats, and matting.

Several forms and materials which are unique to Indonesia are represented in these holdings. Metalwork is primarily used in jewelry, musical instruments, and weaponry; all of which are in the collection. More than 100 painted shadow puppets are also included in these holdings.

MELANESIAN COLLECTION

The Melanesian collection (approximately 5,000 objects) is strongest in material from New Guinea, particularly tapa cloth and weaponry of various kinds. Ceramic production is unique to Melanesia, as well as a small area of Micronesia. The collection contains earthenware examples from both regions.

POLYNESIAN COLLECTION

Polynesian holdings (of approximately 2,500 objects) are strongest in materials from Hawaii and Samoa. Perhaps the most colorful objects in the entire Pacific collection are the feather capes and body ornaments from Polynesia and New Zealand (see New Zealand collection). Other fiber items in this collection include loom-woven textiles decorated with beads, embroidery, and paint along with tapa items.

MICRONESIAN COLLECTION

The Micronesian collection (approximately 1,300 objects) is strongest in material from the Caroline Islands. In addition to many costume items, there are numerous articles of personal adornment. Both carved wooden canoes and canoe paddles are well represented in the Micronesian collection. Examples of native earthenware vessels are also contained in these holdings.

AUSTRALIAN AND NEW ZEALAND COLLECTIONS
The Australian collection (approximately 600 objects) is strongest in bark paintings, body ornaments, and boomerangs. Similarly, New Zealand holdings (approximately 150 objects) contain several feather costume items.

9A6

South American Ethnology Collection

The South American collection (more than 5,000 objects) encompasses materials dating from the late 19th century to the present, from both the tropical forest and the Andean cultures. Holdings are strongest in personal adornments from specific rain forest groups.

TROPICAL FOREST COLLECTION
The tropical forest area of South America includes all or portions of the countries of Brazil, Columbia, Ecuador, Guyana, Paraguay, Peru, and Venezuela. This collection (more than 4,000 objects) includes sizable holdings from the Bintukus, Bororo, Canela, Jivaro, and Wai Wai groups, among others. From these cultures, the best represented form is that of personal adornment. There are armlets, belts, combs, ear danglers, and skirts made of a wide variety of materials: beads, iridescent beetle wings, bones, cordage, gourds, hair, shell, seeds, and teeth. Colorful feather ornaments are numerous and include such items as armbands, belts, dance wands, ear ornaments, fans, headdresses, necklaces, and skirts. In addition to these ornaments, there are representative examples of painted bark cloth masks, textile samples, and weaving materials; these last items are from the Wai Waigroup.

Although several of the collection's basketry containers, primarily quivers, are decorated with feathers, the majority are finely woven but undecorated. Containers of other material include woven fiber bags and nets, incised and stained gourds, and glazed and painted earthenware vessels from the Aguaruna and Chana cultures. The collection also contains several decorative earthenware vessels made in Brazil for the 1876 Centennial Exposition, which illustrate various stages of production.

ANDEAN AND HIGHLAND GROUPS
Andean groups from the highlands of Bolivia, Chile, and Peru are represented in this 900-object collection. Holdings from this mountainous region are strongest in wool textile and costume items. Textile items include complete blankets and unfinished belts showing technique. Articles of costume include a variety of items from knitted caps and decorated hats to belts and ponchos. Personal ornaments in the collection include silver or white metal brooches, earrings, metal-studded hair tapes, pendants, and shawl pins.

9A7

Archeology Collection

The Archeology collection contains more than a million artifacts from the Americas (approximately 90 percent of total holdings) and the Old World, defined as Egypt and the Mediterranean area. There are, in addition, a very few assorted collections from the Orient as well. Although holdings are composed primarily of ceramic sherds, stone flakes, and arrowheads, there are many complete earthenware vessels and figures, stone carvings, and metalwork artifacts. These atypical holdings, although representing only a small proportion of the total collection, still number in the thousands of individual pieces.

MIDDLE AMERICAN AND CARIBBEAN ARCHEOLOGY
The Middle American and Caribbean collection contains decorated earthenware face and figural vessels, from Mexican, Nicaraguan, and Panamanian sites. Holdings also encompass rare anthropomorphic jade carvings, obsidian knives, stone figures, stools, and whorls (fly wheel on a spindle).

SOUTH AMERICAN ARCHEOLOGY
The South American collection contains a significant number of earthenware and figural vessels, some of which are painted, from sites in Brazil, Columbia, Ecuador, and Venezuela.

Holdings from Peruvian sites are large and of diverse materials. The collection includes base and precious metal artifacts, as well as blackwares and earthenwares, some of which are decorated with polychrome. There is a large collection of textile fragments and complete costume and domestic items along with spinning and weaving implements.

NORTH AMERICAN ARCHEOLOGY
The North American archeological collections are strongest in artifacts from the Arctic, Eastern, Midwestern, and Southwestern areas. From Arctic sites are wooden masks, ivory and stone carvings. There are Eastern and Midwestern earthenware vessels, carved soapstone pipes, engraved shells, and a unique collection of wood carvings from Florida. There are large collections of Southwestern earthenware, some painted with zoomorphic and polychrome designs, and stone carvings.

OLD WORLD ARCHEOLOGY
The Old World collection contains Egyptian, Etruscan, Greek, Roman, Middle Eastern, Swiss Lake Dweller, and other assorted artifacts. Egyptian holdings include wooden funerary cases and furniture fragments, faïence figures, jewelry, and vessels; and textile fragments. There are Etruscan, Greek, and Roman painted earthenware vessels, Roman glass and jewelry, as well as similar objects

made of bronze. Middle Eastern artifacts include bronze weapons, coins, stamp seals, cuneiform tablets, ceramic vessels, and tile fragments.

FINDING AIDS
Card catalog arranged by catalog number.
Computerized inventory and index under development.
File will be cross-indexed by culture, provenience, collector/donor, and object name.

SELECTED PUBLICATIONS
Bulletin of the Bureau of American Ethnology. Washington, D.C., Smithsonian Institution. 1879–1965.
Smithsonian Contributions to Anthropology. Washington, D.C., Smithsonian Institution 1965–.
Contributions, which replaces the *Bulletin of the Bureau of American Ethnology*, encompasses a worldwide cultural scope and devotes itself to research areas of the Museum's anthropologists. Publications include illustrations, maps, and tables.

LENDING POLICY
Loans are granted to educational institutions. Permission is dependent on the condition of the specimen and the facilities of the borrowing institution. Approval of the Curator of the appropriate cultural area and the Department Chairman is required. Inquiries should be addressed to the Chairman, Department of Anthropology.

PHOTODUPLICATION SERVICE
Available at prevailing rates, subject to rules and procedures of the Museum. Inquiries should be addressed to the Department of Anthropology.

PUBLIC ACCESS
Exhibition galleries open from 10–5:30 daily except Christmas. Museum hours may be extended between Memorial Day and Labor Day. Research inquiries and requests for information concerning objects not currently on exhibition should be addressed to the

Department of Anthropology
National Museum of Natural History
Smithsonian Institution
Washington, D.C. 20560

9_B

Department of Invertebrate Zoology

The Department of Invertebrate Zoology is concerned with the systematics, distribution, natural history, and ecology of marine and freshwater invertebrates. In addition to the twenty-five million specimens, there are approximately eighty objects which may be of interest to decorative arts historians.

CLASSIFIED CATALOG OF OBJECTS

Costume (Garments and Accessories)
50 shell buttons illustrating the process of buttonmaking; Pacific Island area.
glove woven from the secretions of bivalve Pinna; Mediterranean area.

Jewelry
small collection of jewelry made of shell; Pacific Island area.

Metalwork: Precious Metals
silver tea and punch service with a tridacna shell punch bowl, made in Fernando
Framora's silversmithy for the St. Louis Exposition; Manila, Philippines; 1904.

FINDING AIDS

Card catalog arranged by catalog number.
Computerized catalog of the collection.

LENDING POLICY

Loans are granted to educational institutions. Permission is dependent on the condition of the specimen and the facilities of the borrowing institution. Approval of the Department Chairman and Museum Director is required. Inquiries should be addressed to the Chairman, Department of Invertebrate Zoology.

PHOTODUPLICATION SERVICE

Available at prevailing rates, subject to rules and procedures of Department and Museum. Inquiries should be addressed to the Department of Invertebrate Zoology.

PUBLIC ACCESS

Exhibition galleries open from 10–5:30 daily except Christmas. Museum hours may be extended between Memorial Day and Labor Day. Research inquiries and requests for information concerning objects not currently on exhibition should be addressed to the

Department of Invertebrate Zoology
National Museum of Natural History
Smithsonian Institution
Washington, D.C. 20560

9c

Department of Mineral Sciences

The Department of Mineral Sciences is concerned with the composition and formation of the universe, with special interest in the planet Earth. The origins of extraterrestrial material which has fallen upon it or has been brought back from the Moon by astronauts in the Apollo space program are also of interest to the Department. Areas of study include geology, meteoritics, mineralogy, petrology, and volcanology.

Of the Department's approximately 300,000 specimens, objects of interest to decorative arts historians are primarily found in the gem collection. Forms and materials are eclectic, varying from Chinese jade carvings to Southwestern American Indian jewelry. Notable collections include the Maude Monnell Vetlesen Collection of Chinese jade carvings, given by Edmund C. Monnell in 1959; the American Gemstone Jewelry Collection commissioned by the American Gem Society and designed by Aldo Cipullo, ca. 1978; and a superb gold and gem-encrusted figure of St. George and the Dragon given by Mr. and Mrs. John Levey and Mr. and Mrs. Robert Levey.

CLASSIFIED CATALOG OF OBJECTS

Bibelots and Miniatures
small collection of snuff bottles, boxes, desk sets, figures, and other forms (including pieces attributed to the Fabergé shop); agate, coral, crystal, jade, lapis lazuli, malachite, onyx, shell, slate; various origins and dates.
80 stone animal carvings; carved in Idar-Oberstein, Germany; ca. 1978.
cloisonné enamel and diamond tea service; India; 18th century.
30 small bowls of carved stone by George Ashley; USA; ca. 1950.

Jewelry
25 pieces of jewelry, including state gifts; primarily Europe; 19th and 20th centuries.

Other Materials
small collection of carved ivory; China; pre-1900.
142 jade scepters, plaques, and ceremonial vessels; China; 18th through 20th centuries.

FINDING AIDS
Computerized catalog of the collections.

SELECTED PUBLICATIONS
Desautels, Paul E. Gems in the Smithsonian Institution. 1965. Reprint. Washington, D.C.: Smithsonian Institution Press, 1980.

This illustrated booklet describes the National Gem Collection, the study and shaping of gems, and the principal species.

————. *The Gem Kingdom*. New York: Random House, 1978.

This volume discusses the history, quality, mining, cutting, and setting of gemstones. The collection's carved jades and royal jewelry are included and illustrated.

LENDING POLICY

Loans are granted to educational institutions. Permission is dependent on the condition of the specimen and the facilities of the borrowing institution. Approval of the Department Chairman and Museum Director required. Inquiries should be addressed to the Chairman, Department of Mineral Sciences.

PHOTODUPLICATION SERVICE

Available at prevailing rates, subject to rules and procedures of the Department and Museum. Inquiries should be addressed to the Department of Mineral Sciences.

PUBLIC ACCESS

Exhibition galleries open from 10–5:30 daily except Christmas. Museum hours may be extended between Memorial Day and Labor Day. Research inquiries and requests for information concerning objects not currently on exhibition should be addressed to the

Curator of Minerals and Gems
National Museum of Natural History
Smithsonian Institution
Washington, D.C. 20560

10

National Portrait Gallery

The National Portrait Gallery, established by an Act of Congress in 1962, collects, exhibits, and studies portraits of "men and women who have made significant contributions to the history, development, and culture of the people of the United States, and of artists who created such portraits." The Gallery is housed in the Patent Office Building, designed by Robert Mills, Thomas Ustick Walter, and William Parker Elliot in 1836 and opened to the public as the National Portrait Gallery in 1968.

As an art, biography, and history museum, the Gallery holds approximately 9,000 portraits in the media of drawing, painting, photography, prints, sculpture, and silhouette. Collections also include twenty-five decorative arts objects either associated with the sitters represented in the portrait collection or used as furnishings for the Gallery.

33 Tea service, 1931.
Made in the Georg Jensen Silversmithy, Denmark.
Silver with ivory handles.

34 Pitcher, 1808(?).
    Liverpool, England.
    Silhouette of the Reverend Absalom
    Jones.
    Creamware.

The National Portrait Gallery also administers the Catalog of American Portraits (CAP). A national reference center, the CAP's files contain photographs and documentation for more than 60,000 likenesses of historically important Americans as well as portraits by noteworthy American artists. While painting, sculpture, and drawing are the most common media included in the files, images of other forms (ceramics, medals, plaques, textiles, and other media) are also collected not only because they are derived from the fine arts, but because their iconographic value is of scholarly interest. The CAP additionally maintains a supplementary photographic file of dated portraits. Arranged chronologically, this file provides a unique reference tool for the study of American costume, interiors, decorative arts, and other subjects.

CLASSIFIED CATALOG OF OBJECTS

Ceramics
creamware pitcher decorated with transfer-printed portrait of Absalom Jones;
    Liverpool, England; ca. 1808.

Furniture
20 pieces of furniture including a suite designed by Victor Proetz; England, USA;
    17th through 20th centuries.

Heating Devices
cast iron fireplace stove; USA; ca. 1820.

Metalwork: Precious Metal
5-piece silver tea service made by Georg Jensen Silversmithy; Denmark; ca. 1931.

FINDING AIDS
Card catalog arranged by accession number.

LENDING POLICY
Loans are granted to educational institutions for exhibition. Loans must be approved by the Museum Director.

PHOTODUPLICATION SERVICE
Available at prevailing rates subject to rules and procedures of the Gallery. Inquiries should be addressed to the Office of the Curator, National Portrait Gallery.

PUBLIC ACCESS
Exhibition galleries open from 10–5:30 daily except Christmas. Museum hours may be extended between Memorial Day and Labor Day. Research inquiries and information concerning objects not currently on exhibition write to

Office of the Curator
National Portrait Gallery
Smithsonian Institution
Washington, D.C. 20560

11

Office of Horticulture

The Office of Horticulture is responsible for the development and management of the grounds and interior plantings of the Smithsonian Institution as botanical and horticultural exhibition areas and for carrying out research on various aspects of horticultural history. The Office is also concerned with both mid-19th and early 20th century American garden furnishings and with Christmas tree ornaments. The tree ornaments are on view only during the annual "Trees of Christmas" exhibition. There are more than 7,000 contemporary handmade ornaments representing various national cultures (Brazil, Denmark, Italy, Japan, and Poland), materials and techniques (cookies, decoupage, painted porcelain, gold thread embroidery, and origami), and various themes (American Victorian, childhood, and the Twelve Days of Christmas).

35   Garden bench, ca. 1860.
     Wire.

CLASSIFIED CATALOG OF OBJECTS

Furniture

130 pieces of cast iron garden furniture, fountains, and works in ornamental wire (including pieces by J.W. Fiske, Fred Gensel & Co., Kramer Bros., J. McLean, J.L. Mott, Peter Timmes & Son); USA; mid- to late 19th century.

FINDING AIDS

Card catalog arranged by accession number.

LENDING POLICY

Loans are granted to educational institutions for exhibition. Loans must be approved by the Director of Horticulture and are subject to review by the Assistant Secretary for Museum Programs. An information sheet is available from the Office of Horticulture, Research and Education Division, Arts and Industries Building.

PHOTODUPLICATION SERVICE

Available at prevailing rates, subject to rules and procedures of the Office of Horticulture. Inquiries should be addressed to the Office of Horticulture.

PUBLIC ACCESS

Research inquiries and for information concerning objects not currently on exhibition, write to the

Office of Horticulture, Research and Education Division
Arts and Industries Building
Smithsonian Institution
Washington, D.C. 20560

36   Garden urn, ca. 1880.
     Cast iron.

12

Smithsonian Institution Archives

The Smithsonian Institution Archives collects, preserves, and makes available to researchers, the history of the Smithsonian Institution. The collection contains official records and photographs of the Smithsonian Institution; correspondence and photographs concerning the construction and history of the museum buildings; papers of the Secretaries; taped interviews with selected staff members; papers and research notes of the staff in the fields of art, history, humanities, and science; records and photographs pertaining to major international expositions; and records relating to special collections, museum exhibitions, and donors. Decorative arts researchers may be particularly interested in drawings

37 Smithsonian Institution Building, un-
    dated.
    Photograph.

and blueprints of Smithsonian Institution buildings, and photographs of both in-house and international exhibitions.

The Archives also conducts a program in the administration of archive and manuscript collections.

FINDING AIDS
The following *Guide* describes more than 400 collections in the Archives.
Guide to the Smithsonian Archives, 1978. Washington, D.C.: Smithsonian Institution Press, 1978.
Finding aids to some collections available in the Archives.

PHOTODUPLICATION SERVICE
Policies and costs of reproduction dependent on whether the documents are on microfilm. An updated list of Smithsonian archives on microfilm is available. Write to the Smithsonian Institution Archives.

PUBLIC ACCESS
Information requests and reference inquiries should be addressed to the

Smithsonian Institution Archives
Arts and Industries Building
Smithsonian Institution
Washington, D.C. 20560

38 Arts and Industries Building decorated
    for the James A. Garfield-Chester A.
    Arthur Inaugural Ball, 1881.
    Photograph.

13

Smithsonian Institution Furnishings Collection

The red seneca sandstone Norman Revival-style Smithsonian Institution Building was designed by James Renwick, Jr., in 1846 and completed in 1855. Although a serious fire in January 1865 destroyed the second floor and three of the Castle's largest towers, the exterior restoration faithfully follows Renwick's plans. However, with the exception of the Great Hall and the Commons, all of the building's principal rooms have been changed during the four alterations which have been necessary since the 1865 fire.

The Castle houses the administrative headquarters of the Smithsonian Institution and the Woodrow Wilson International Center for Scholars.

The Smithsonian Institution Furnishings Collection was established in 1964 to collect 19th century furnishings to be used in the principal offices and reception rooms of the original building and in the Arts and Industries Building (1879). Although this 2,300-object collection contains primarily American furniture dating from 1840 to 1880, there are numerous examples from both earlier and later periods. Craftsmen and designers represented in the collection include Moore and Campion, James Renwick, Jr., Henry Hobson Richardson, Alexander Roux, and Isaac Vose. A large collection of mid-to late 19th century gas lighting devices is also of note to decorative arts historians.

CLASSIFIED CATALOG OF OBJECTS

Architectural Elements
architectural model of the Smithsonian Institution Building made by James Renwick, Jr.; USA; 1847.
2 painted canvas panels, designed by Louis Sullivan for the Chicago Stock Exchange; USA; ca. 1875–80.

Ceramics
30 pieces of Rihouet porcelain tablewares; France; ca. 1840.

Furniture
1,600 pieces of furniture including office forms; England, France, primarily USA; ca. 1840–80.

Lighting Devices
70 gas chandeliers and lamps; USA; ca. 1850–80.

Metalwork: Precious Metals
Smithsonian Institution gold badge and silver mace, both designed by Leslie Durbin; London; 1965.

39   Arm chair, ca. 1845.
     USA.
     Walnut.

Timepieces and Measuring Devices
small collection of mantel clocks; France, primarily USA; ca. 1870–90.

Textiles
tapestry; Flanders; seventeenth century.

FINDING AIDS
Card catalog arranged by catalog number.
Curatorial notebooks arranged by location and type of object.

LENDING POLICY
Loans are granted to other museums and educational institutions for exhibition.
Loans must be approved by the Special Assistant to The Secretary.

PHOTODUPLICATION SERVICE
Available at prevailing rates, subject to rules and procedures of the Smithsonian
Institution Furnishings Collection. Inquiries should be addressed to the keeper
of the Smithsonian Institution Building.

PUBLIC ACCESS
The Smithsonian Institution Building, which houses the Main Information Center for the Smithsonian Institution, is open from 10–5:30 daily except Christmas.
Hours may be extended between Memorial Day and Labor Day. The Collection
is housed in the office area of the building which is not open to the public.
Requests for appointments to see the collection and for curatorial information
should be addressed to the

Keeper of the Smithsonian Institution Building
Smithsonian Institution
Washington, D.C. 20560

INDEX

Arabic numerals and alphanumerics refer to collection descriptions. The Index is a single alphabetical list that includes the following information drawn from the collection descriptions:

all corporate, geographic, and personal names that occur in the collection descriptions

all object types and materials that occur in the collection descriptions (e.g., *inrō*, furniture, lacquer)

subjects specifically mentioned in the collection descriptions (e.g., costume industry; medical science, history of)

titles of works cited in the collection descriptions

titles of publications cited in the collection descriptions

all authors included in the bibliographic entries

The Index does not include titles of publications listed in the bibliographic entries.

Abyssinia 9A
Acoma 9A4
Adrian 8D
Advertising design 2, 8A
Advertising, history of American 8A
Afghanistan 3E, 9A2
Africa 2A, 4, 5, 8C, 9A1. See also specific country. See also specific culture.
African-American material 8B, 8C
Agate, carved 2A, 8L, 9C
Agricultural implements 9A2
Agriculture, history of American 8G
Aguaruna 9A6
Air Force One (Presidential aircraft) 6
Air pump 8Q
Akua ba (doll) 4
Alabaster, carved 4, 7C, 9A2
Albers, Anni 1
Aleut 9A4

Alexandria, Virginia 8E
Algeria 9A1
Altar linens 9A2. See also Religious material. See also Textiles
Aluminium 2A, 6
Amber, carved 2A
Amelung, John Frederick 8B
American Gemstone Jewelry Collection 9C
American Gem Society 9C
American Indians. See North American Indians
American material. See USA
American Pharmaceutical Association 8L
American Porcelain: New Expressions in an Ancient Art 7
Americans, famous 8R
Americans, objects associated with famous 8R
Amlash 4

Anatolia 4
Angoulême 6
Amhara 9A1
Amphora 8C
Amulets 3E. See also Ornaments
Andaman and Nicobar Islands 9A2
Andes and highlands (South America)
    9A6. See also specific country
Angell, Joseph, III 2A
Angola 9A1
Animal-powered vehicles 8T
Animals, study of 9
Animals (subject heading, Cooper-Hewitt
    Museum Library Picture Collection) 2
Anklets 9A5. See also Ornaments
Anthropology 9A, 9A4
Anti-war movement 8R
Apache 9A4
Apollo (Space craft) 6, 9C
Apothecaries 8L
Apothecary jars 8L
Applied work (Textile) 9A4
Arabia 9A2
Arapaho 9A4
Archeology collections 8, 8B, 8O, 9A, 9A7
Architectural elements 2
  Africa 5
  Austria 2A
  Bohemia 2A
  Canada 8C
  China 2A
  Egypt 2A
  England 2A, 8T
  Europe 7C. See also under specific coun-
    try
  France 2A
  Germany 2A, 8L
  India 2A
  Indian Subcontinent 9A2
  Indonesia 2A
  Iran 2A
  Italy 2A
  Japan 2A, 3C
  Netherlands 2A
  Pacific Islands 9A5
  Russia 2A
  Spain 2A
  Sweden 2A
  Taiwan 9A2
  Thailand 2A
  Siam. See under Architectural elements,
    Thailand
  USA 2A, 3A, 4, 7C, 8C, 8E, 8F, 8L, 8R,
    8T
Architectural fittings 2A
Architectural model 7C, 13
Architecture, books on 2

Architecture, designs for 2
Archival collections 1, 2, 5, 7A, 8A, 8O,
    8R, 9A, 10, 12
Archives of American Art 1
Arctic (North American Indians) 9A4, 9A7
Argillite, carved 9A4
Armbands. See Ornaments
Armenia 9A2
Armlets. See Ornaments
Arms and armor 2
  Asia 9A2
  Europe 8M, 8O
  USA 8M, 8O
  See also Weapons. See also Edged weap-
    ons
Arrowheads, archeological 9A7
Arrows. See Weapons
Art glass 8B
Arthur Collection, James 8K
Artists, archival material of American 1
Art medals 8U
Art museums 3, 4, 5, 7, 10
Art of North American Indians 9A4
Art organizations, archives of 1
Art pottery 2A, 3A, 8B
Arts and Industries Building 6, 13
Art watches 8K. See also Jewelry. See also
    Watches
Ashanti 4, 9A1
Ashley, George 9C
Asia
  archeology 9A7
  costume (garments and accessories) 8G
  ethnology 9A2
  furniture 8R
  glass 8B
  leatherwork 8G
  needlework 2B, 9A2
  vessels 8B
  See also specific country
Assam 9A2
Astrolabes 8I
Astronomical instruments 8Q
Athabascan, Northern 9A4
Atil, Esin 3, 3E
Atom smashers 8
Augsburg 2A
Australia 6, 9A5
Austria 2A, 7C
Automat. See Horn and Hardart Automat
Automata 8K, 8N. See also Timepieces and
    measuring devices
Aviation, history of American 6

Badges (political) 8R
Bags
  Africa 9A1

LOCATION GUIDE
TO ARTISTS, DESIGNERS, MAKERS, MANUFACTURERS, PRODUCTION CENTERS, AND RETAILERS

The Location Guide to Artists, Designers, Makers, Manufacturers, Production Centers, and Retailers is a computer-generated alphabetical listing of all such names represented in eight major decorative arts collections of the Smithsonian Institution: Cooper-Hewitt Museum, Department of Decorative Arts and Department of Wallpaper; National Museum of American Art; and the following divisions of the National Museum of American History: Division of Ceramics and Glass, Division of Community Life, Division of Costume, Division of Domestic Life, Division of Musical Instruments, and Division of Textiles.

The names in the Location Guide were compiled from the internal files of these eight major decorative arts collections. Because of limitations imposed by the computer, diacritical marks do not appear. Every effort has been made to standardize the spelling of names and the alphabetical ordering of names with articles where there was spelling variation from collection to collection; however, errors may still exist in the list. Corrections to names and additional information about partially identified names will be gratefully accepted from users of the *Guide*.

The Location Guide is a list indicating in which of the eight major decorative arts collections these names can be found. The Location Guide does not function as an index for the material in this volume.

The alphanumeric designations are as follows:

2   Cooper-Hewitt Museum, Department of Decorative Arts
     and Department of Wallpaper

7   National Museum of American Art

     National Museum of American History
8B   Division of Ceramics and Glass
8C   Division of Community Life
8D   Division of Costume
8E   Division of Domestic Life
8N   Division of Musical Instruments
8S   Division of Textiles

A. 2, 8B, 8E
A.A. 8E
Aalto, Alvar 2
Aansworth Ltd. 8D
A.B. 8B, 8E
Abbot, John W. 8E
A.B.D. 8E
Abercrombie & Fitch Co. 8D
Abraham & Strauss 8D
Absalom, William 8D
A.C. 8E
Acking, Carl-Axel 2
A. & Co. 8E
A.C.O. 8E
Acton, R.C. 8E
A.D. 8E
Adam Bros. 2
Adam, Johann Jacob 2
Adam, John 8E
Adams 2, 8B
Adams, Chandler & Co. 8E
Adams Clothes 8D
Adams & Co. 2, 8B
Adams, Desy & London 2
Adams, E.B. 8E
Adams, George W. 7
Adams, Herbert 2
Adams, Pygan 8E
Adams, R.L. 8E
Adams, Stephen 2
Adams, Stephen, Sr. 8E
Adams, William 2, 8B
Adams, William, & Co. 8E
Adams, William, & Sons 8B
Adams, William W. 8E
Addaar 8D
Adelphi Silverplate Co. 8E
Adler 8D
Adolfo 8D
Adrian 8D
Adriance 8E
A.D.S. 2
A.E. 8E
Aeolian Co. 8N
A.E.W. 8E
A.F. 8E
A.F. & Co. 8E
Agenzia Campana 8B
A.G.F. 8E
A.G.M. Co. 8E
Agry, J.B.M. 2
Aguado, Deborah 7
A.H. 8E
A.H.H. 2

Ahrens, Therese 8D
A.I. 8E
A.I.C. 8E
Aiken, George 8E
Aiken, Lambert & Co. 8E
Ainsworth, Albert 2
Aitken, Robert 2
A.I. V.K. 2
A.J. 2
A. & J.Z. 8E
A.K. 8E
Akao School 2
Akao Yoshitsugu 2
Akasaka 2
Akasaka-Higo School 2
Akasaka School 2
Akasaka Tadashige 2
Akio Giokuseido 2
Akitoshi 2
A.L. 8E
Albert 2, 8E
Alberti, Johann Philip, & Horan, Johann Christian 8E
Albert Originals 8D
Albrecht, C.F.L. 8N
Albrecht, Charles 8N
Alcock, A. 8B
Alcock, John 8B
Alcock, S. 8B
Alcock, Samuel, & Co. 8B
Alcora 2, 8B
Aldrich, Larry 8D
Alessandrodi Milano 8D
Alexander 8D
Alexander, J. 8E
Alexander, Violet Elizabeth Lee 8S
Alfred 2
Algeo, C.C. 8E
Allain, Francois 8E
Allebone 8D
Allen 2
Allen, Bob 8D
Allen Cutlery Co. 8E
Allen-Higgins Co. 2
Allen-Higgins W.P. Co. 2
Allen, John 8E
Allen, John P. 8C
Allen, J.P., Co. 8D
Allen, William, Originals 8D
Allien, Henry V., & Co. 2
Allien, H.V., & Co. 2
Allowaystown, New Jersey 8B
Altman, B., & Co. 8D

Altman, Bechard 8D
Alvin 8E
A.M. 8B, 8E
A.M.A. 8N
Amalfi 8D
Aman, Georg 8N
Amburgey, Jethro 8N
A.M. & C. 2
A.M. & Cie 2
Amelung, John Frederick 8B
America Historical Plate 8B
American Bisque Porcelain, Inc. 8B
American Chair Co. 8E
American China Co. 8B
American China Manufactory 8B
American Numismatic Society 2
American Piano Co. 8N
American Pottery Co. 8B
American Silver Co. 8E
American Sterling Co. 8E
American Wallpaper Manufacturers Assoc. 2
American Waltham Watch Co. 8D
Ames, Arthur 7
Amies, Hardy 8D
Amigoni, Jacopo 2
Amman, Erhard 8N
Ammann & Bitzer 8D
Ampico 8N
Amstel 8B
Amsterdam 8B
Amy 8D
Anchor Hocking Glass Co. 8B
Anderson, Don 8D
Anderson Studio 8E
Andreasen, Jens 2
Andreoli, Giorgio 2
Andrews, A.H., & Co. 8E
Andrieu 8B
Andrieu, Bertrand 2
An-Ev 8D
Angell, Joseph 2
Anglo Fabric Co., Inc. 8D
Angouleme 8B
Angulo, M. 8E
Anker, Albert 2
Annapolis, Maryland 8B
Anna Pottery 8B
Ansbach 8B
Ansonia 8D

Beyde, August 8N
Beyrouth, Syria 8B
B.F. 2
B.F.B. 8B
B. & H. 7, 8E
B.H.B. Co. 8E
Bickley 2
Bickmin, Dorothy 8D
Bien Jolie 8D
Bigelow, J.J. 8E
Bigelow, Kennard & Co. 8E
Billings, William 8E
Billon, Charles 8E
Billotey 2
Biloxi Art Pottery 8B
Bilston 2
Biltmore Clothes 8D
Bilton, Richard John 8N
Binckert 2
Bing & Grondahl 2, 8B
Binghamton Chair Co. 7
Binns, Charles Fergus 8B
Birdseye 8D
Birge, M.H. Co. 2
Birks 8E
Birks, A. 8B
Birmingham 2
Bishop, Mary Ann 8S
Bissell, George E. 2
Bivens, Daniel 8C
Bjorkman, Roy R. 8D
Blackburn, W. 8C
Blackford 8E
Blackinton, R., & Co. 8D, 8E
Blackman, John Starr 8E
Black, Starr & Frost 8E
Blagden, Hodgson & Co. 8E
Blaich, Robert 2
Blair, James E. 8C
Blake, James E., Co. 8E
Blanc, Victor 8E
Bland, John 8N
Blass, Bill 8D
Blenko Glass Co. 7
Blitz Olympic 8D
Block, Fred A. 8D
Blondel, John, & Co. 8E
Bloomingdale's 8D
Bloor, William 8B
Blowers, John 8E
Blum, H. 8D
Blumrich, Stephen 7
Blynn & Baldwin 8E
B.M. 8B, 8E

Boardman & Hart 2, 8E
Boardman, Sherman 8E
Boardman, Thomas D. & Sherman 8E
Bobe, J.B., & Co. 8E
Bock, Franz 8N
Bockstrom, Monica 8B
Boch, William, & Bros. 8B
Boda 2, 8B
Boehm 2
Boehm & Boehm 2
Boehm, Edward Marshall 8B
Boeklage, William 8D
Boelen, Jacob 8E
Bohland & Fuchs 8N
Bohm & Mendler 8N
Boisette 8B
Bole, H. Barbezat 2
Bollander, L.P., & Co. 8D
Bomart Music Co. 8N
Bombaugh, Calvin 8B
Bomke, Valentijn Casper 2
Bond 8D
Bondie, Edith 7
Bond, Judy 8D
Bonettus, Pretrus 8N
Bonhop, Paul, Toys Inc. 2
Boni 8N
Bon Marche Dry Goods Co. 2
Bonnardot & Cie 2
Bonnetain, A. 2
Bonnet, J.M. 8E
Bonnie Doon 8D
Bonnin & Morris 8B
Bononien, Ionnes Baptista 8N
Bon Ton, The 8D
Bonwit Teller 8D
Boonton Ware 2
Boote, T. & R. 8B
Booth, L., & Sons 8E
Bordillon 8E
Borgila, Atelier 2
Bornhoeft 8N
Borocco 8E
Borsalino 8D
Bosch, Dennis 7
Bose Corp. 8N
Bosello, Domenico 2
Bosphorus, Turkey 8B
Bossart, Karl 2
Bosse, Abraham 2
Bosstone Co. 8N
Boston Earthenware Mfg. & Co. 8B

Boston Musical Instrument Manufactory 8N
Boston & Sandwich Glass Co. 2, 8B
Boswell, William 2
Botany 8D
Bottger, Johann Friedrich 8B
Bouchardon 2
Boucher 2
Boucheron 2
Boudin, Leonard 2
Boudo, Louis 8E
Bouillat, Francois 2
Boulanget, F. 8E
Boullemier, A. 8B
Boullt, T.A. 8E
Boulton, M., & Co. 8E
Boulton & Watt 2
Bouraine 2
Bourdois 2
Bourgeois, George 2
Bourg-La-Reine 2
Bourne, J., & Sons, Ltd. 8B
Bouvet 2
Bouy, Jules 2
Bow 2, 8B
Bowen, John 2
Bowen, Louis W., Inc. 2
Bower, S. & B. 8E
Bowers, W.H. 8E
Bowring Arunel & Co. 8D
Boyce, Geradus 8E
Boyce, John 8E
Boyden & Fenno 8E
Boyd, Parks 8E
Boyd-Richardson 8D
Boynton, Calvin 8B
Boynton, C., & Co. 8B
Boynton, R. Ellsworth 8B
Bozen 8B
B.P. 8B
B.R. 2
Brachard 2
Brachard, Jean-Charles-Nicolas 2
Brackett, Abbie Corey 8S
Bradbury, Theophilus 8E
Bradford, Cornelius 8E
Bradley 8D
Bradley, Frederick 2
Bradley & Hubbard 8E
Bradstone 8D
Brady, William 8E
Braendli & Co. 2
Brager, B.B. 2

Brainard, Elizabeth 8E
Bramah 8D
Bramah, J. 2
Brammell, Mary Tilton 8B
Bramsche, Rash & Co. 2
Branch 8D
Brandt, Edgar 2
Brannam, Devon 8B
Brannan, Daniel 8B, 8C
Brasher, Ephriam 8E
Braun, A.G. 2
Braverman & Levy 8E
Bray, Sollace & Dauchy 8E
Breads 8D
Bregnet 2
Breininger, Barbara 8B
Breininger, Lester P. 8B
Brelsford, J. 8B
Bremond 8N
Brenet, Nicolas Guy 2
Brenner, Victor David 2
Brental & Hall 8D
Brenton, Benjamin 8E
Breuer, Marcel 2
Brevoort, John 8E
Brewster, George T. 2
Briddell, Donald C. 7
Bridgeport Silver Co. 8E
Bridgetown, New Jersey
    8B
Briel, Michael, & Krieger,
    J.G. 8E
Brigance, Tom 8D
Brigden, Timothy 8E
Brigden, Zachariah 8E
Briggs, Cornelius 8E
Briggs, D.F., Co. 8D
Bristol 2, 8B
Bristol Mfg. Co. 8E
Bristol Plate Co. 8E
British-American House
    8D
Brizzi & Nicolai 8N
Broadwood, Johannes 8N
Broadwood, John, & Sons
    8N
Broderip 8N
Brodhead, Dorothy 2
Brogan, Thomas F. 8E
Brooks, Bobbie 8D
Brooks Bros. 8D
Brooks, Donald 8D
Brocks, George 7
Brooks, Mona 7
Brooks, Romaine 7
Broome, Isaac 8B
Brother Thomas of Wes-

ton Priory 8B
Brouwer, Theophilus A.
    8B
Brown, D. 8E
Brown, E. 8E
Browne & Seal 8E
Brownfield, William, &
    Sons 8B
Brown Hatter 8D
Brownhill's Pottery Co. 8B
Brown, J.G.K. 2
Brown, J.L. 8E
Brown-Jordan Co. 2
Brown, Mahala 8S
Brown-Westhead, Moore,
    & Co. 8B
Brunias, Agostino 2
Bruno 8N
Brunstrom, J.A. 8E
Brunt, Henry 8B
Bruria 7
Bruschi, Gaspare 2
Brussels 8B
Bryan, Ann Elizabeth
    King 8D
Bryan & Co. 8D
Bryan, Harriet C. 2
Bryce Bros. 8B
Bryce, Walker & Co. 8B
B.S. 8B, 8E
Buchanan, James 8E
Bucherer 8D
Buckingham 8C
Buckingham & Hecht 8D
Buck, Jacob 8B
Buckley, Oliver 8E
Buckner, William 8C
Buckwalter, Francis, &
    Co. 8E
Budworth, J. 8E
Buen Retiro 2, 8B
Buffalo Pottery 8B
Buffams' 8D
Buffet Crampon & Co. 8N
Buhner & Keller 8N
Buleigh, Sydney R. 8E
Bullin 8E
Bullock, Daniel 8B
Bullock's Wilshire 8D
Bundza, Janis 8N
Bunel 8E
Burden, Joseph 8E
Burdines 8D
Burger, John 8E
Burgess, H. 8B
Burgues, Irving C. 8B
Burgundy 8B

Burkart, F.R. 8N
Burke, Charles C. 2
Burkhard, Peter 8E
Burlington 8D
Burnett, Charles A. 8E
Burpee, Jeremiah, Pottery
    8B
Burr 8E
Burr, C. 8E
Burrows, Alice & George
    8E
Burrows, Stephen 8D
Burr, Stanford S. 8E
Burt, Arthur 8D
Burt, Benjamin 8E
Burt, John 8E
Burton's 8D
Burt, Samuel 8E
Burt, William 8E
Bushu Kinai School 2
Bushu School 2
Bushu Sunagawa School 2
Busse, Jane 7
Buster Brown 8D
Busvines, Ltd. 8D
Buthaud, Rene 8B
Butler, Frances 7
Butler, James 8E
Butler Shop 8E
Butt, R. 8B
B. & V.B. 8E
B.V. E.T. 2
B.V.R. 8E
B.W. 8E
B.W.C. Co. 8D
B. & W. Co. 8D
B.W.M. & Co. 8B
Byles, Thomas 8E
Byng, Valentyn 2
Byrnes, George & Co. 2
Byron, Charles B., Co. 8E

C. 2, 8B, 8E
C.A. 2
Cacharel 8D
Cadillac 8D
Cadwallader, Brooke 8D
Cage, Xenia 2
Cahier, J. Charles 2
Caillard, Robert 2
Cain, A. 2
Cain, Auguste 2
Calder, Alexander 2, 7
Calder, Stirling 2
Calder, William 8E
Caldor's 8D
Caldwell, Edward F., &

Works 8B
Chicago United Wallpaper
  Co. 2
Chickering 8N
Chien, J. 8E
Childers, Philip 7
Children's Motivational
  Environments, Inc. 7
Childs, Otis 8E
Chimu Culture (Peru) 2
Chino, Marie Z. 7
Chiparus, Demetre 2
Chippendale, Thomas 2
Chiswick, Chateau 8B
Chittenango Pottery 8B
Chizuka Hisanori 2
Chloe 8D
Chobei Kiku 2
Choisy-le-Roi 2, 8B
Chollar, Thomas D. 8B
Choshu 2
Choshu Hagi, Okamoto
  School 2
Choshu Hagi School 2
Choshu Harumasa 2
Choshu, Okamoto School
  2
Choshu School 2
Choy, Katherine 2
Christine 8D
Christofle 2, 7
Christofle & Cie 8E
Christoph 8N
Cin-Cabinet Co. 8E
Cincinnati, Ohio 8B
Cindy Kay 8D
Cipolla, Salvatore 8B
Cira 8D
City Pottery Co. 8B
Claiborne, Liz 8D
Clair Munson 8E
Clancy, M.E. 8D
Clanton, Harry A. 8B
Clapp, Edwin, & Sons,
  Inc. 8D
Clark 8E
Clark, Atkins A. 8E
Clark, B.A., & Co. 8E
Clark, Decius 8B
Clark, Decius W., & Ly-
  man, Alanson Potter
  8B
Clarke, E. 8B
Clarke, Edward 8B
Clarke, Jonathan 8E
Clark, Forbes 8E
Clark & Fox 8B

Clark, Francis 8E
Clark, G.G. 8E
Clark, Nathan, & Co. 8B
Clark, Nathan, & Fox,
  Ethan S. 8B
Clark, Nathan, Jr. 8B
Clark, Peter 8B
Clawson Iron Foundry 7
Clear, Richard 8B
Clementi & Co. 8N
Clementi, Muzio, & Co.
  8N
Clementson, Joseph 8B
Clem & Lee 8D
Clendenin, W. 8N
Clerissy 2
Cleveland, B. 8E
Cleveland, William 8E
Clews, James 8B
Clews, Ralph 8B
Clichy 8B
Clifton Art Pottery 8B
Clignancourt 8B
Clin, A. 8D
Clippinger, George 8E
Clodion, Claude-Michel
  8B
Cloos, George 8N
Clothier, Edward 8D
Clough, Ebenezer 2
Clowes & Gates Mfg. Co.
  8E
Cluett, Peabody & Co.,
  Inc. 8D
C.M.L. 2
C.M.U. 8E
C.O. 2
Coalbrookdale 2, 8B
Coalport 2, 8B
Cobb, Ephriam 8E
Cobb's Shoe Store 8D
Coblentz 8D
Cobner, Coomes & Dob-
  bie, Ltd. 8D
Coburn, John 8E
Cochran, M.B. 8C
Cocker, George 2
Cockerill 8N
Cockson & Seddon 8B
Coe, H.A. 8E
Coe, Susan Ann Camp 8S
Cohen, Harriet 7
Cohen, I.B. 8D
Cole 8B
Colebrookdale Furnace 8E
Cole, Esther 8D
Cole of California 8D

Coles, Albert 8D, 8E
Cole & Sons, Ltd. 2
Collaert, Hans 2
Collard & Collard 8N
Collingnon 8E
Collins & Fairbands 8D
Colman, Alex 8D
Colombo, Joe 2
Colonial Co. 8B
Colonial Company Potters
  8B
Colonial Williamsburg,
  Inc. 2
Colorado Springs, Colo-
  rado 8B
Columbia Glass Co. 8B
Columbia Graphophone
  Co. 8N
Columbian Art Pottery 8B
Coman, Molly 2
Commereau, Thomas H.
  8B
Compiegne, Chateau De
  8B
Conn, Charles G. 8N
Conn & Dupont 8N
Connolly Saddle Store 8D
Conoy Springwater Corp.
  8B
Constable, W.H. 8B
Converse 8C, 8D
Cook, B.A., & Co. 2
Cook, Erastus 8E
Cook & Hancock 8B
Cook, John 8E
Cook, Joseph 8E
Cook, Lia 7
Cook Pottery Co. 8B
Cooley, Esther 8S
Coors Porcelain Co. 8B
Copco, Inc. 7
Cope 8E
Copeland 8B
Copeland & Garrett 2
Copeland, William Taylor
  8B
Copeland, W. T. 2, 8B
Copeland, W. T., & Sons 7
Copenhagen 2, 8B
Coppes Bros. & Zook 8E
Copp, Mary C. 8S
Coquerel et le gros a Paris
  8B
Coralie 8D
Corbett, John 8E
Cordier, A. 2
Cordier Freres 2

Doccia 2, 8B
Dodd, Edward, II 8N
Dodd, John 8N
Dodd, Thomas, I 8N
Dodge, F.B. 8E
Dodge, Nehemiah 8E
Dodge Pottery 8B
Dodworth, H.B. 8N
Doeuillet, G. 8D
Dolbeare, Edmund 8E
Dolbeare, J. 8E
Dole, D.N. 8E
Doll, Jacob 8N
Dolmetsch, Ltd. 8N
Dolton, G. 8N
Domard, Joseph-Francois 2
Domley, Charles 8D
Donadieu Modes 8D
Donadio, Angelo 2
Donaghho, Alexander P. 8B
Donaldson, David 8B
Donath, P., Porcelain Factory 8B
Donavan's Irish Manufacture 8B
Done, Joshua 8N
Donn & Co. 8E
Donnelly Terra Cotta Co. 8B
Donovan, John 8B
Don Pottery 8B
Doraku 2
Dorchester Pottery 8B
Dore Superfin Vg 2
Dorn, Marion 2
Dorn, Marion V. 2
Dorsey, Joshua 8E
Doucet, M. 8D
Doughty, Dorothy 8B
Doulton & Co., Ltd. 2, 8B
Dourne 8B
Dover 8D
Dowd, J.B. 8C
Dow, J.M. 8E
D.P. 8E
Dragsten, A. 8E
Draper, Dorothy 2
Draper, Francis 8E
Drentwett, Abraham 2
Dresden 2, 8B
Dresser, Christopher 2
Dreyfous, M. 2
Dreyfuss, Henry 2
Drinkhouse, J. 8E
D'Ritter 8D

Driver 8D
Drouet, L. 8N
Droz, Jean Pierre 2
Dru, Ellen 8D
D.S. 8E
D.S.F. Co. 8E
Duban, Louis Jacques 2
Dubois & Couturier 8N
Dubois, Jean Joseph 2
Dubois, Paul 2
Dubois & Stodart 8N
Dubois, Tunis D. 8E
Dubuffet 2
Ducommun-Girod 2
Dufossee, Succ. De Melnotte 8D
Dufour, Jean Baptist 2
Dufour, Joseph 2
Dufour & Leroy 2
Duhme 8E
Du Berri 8B
Dulcken, Johannes Daniel 8N
Dumarest, Rambert 2
Dumas, Paul 2
Dumont-Noirtin, Louis 8N
Dumoutet, John B. 8E
Dunand, Jean 2
Dunbar Furniture Co. 2
Duncan, George, & Sons 8B
Dunderdale, David 8B
Dunham, Rufus 8E
Dunlap & Co. 8D
Dunn 8N
Dunne, F.L. 8D
Dunn, John 8E
Dunn, Tirzah 2
Duntze, J. 8B
Duofold, Inc. 8D
Du Paquier, Claudius Innocentius 8B
Dupont 8D, 8N
Dupre, Augustin 2
Dupre, Tournai 8N
Dupuy, Daniel 8E
D'Urbino 2
Durgin, F.A. 8E
Durgin, William B., Co. 8E
Durham Duplex Razor Co. 8D
Durham Mfg. Co. 8C
Durlach 8B
Durner, Carolyn 8D
Duro 2

Durosey, Sophie 8B
Dutchmaid 8D
Duvelleroy, J. 8D
Duvivier, Benjamin 2
Duvivier, Jean 2
Duzan, Jane Nelson 8S
Dyott & Kent 2
Dyottville Glass Works 2
Dyrebye, W. 8E

E.A. 8D
Eagle Knit 8D
Eaglesham Accessories 2
Eakins, George 8E
Eames 2
Eames, Charles 2
Eames, Charles & Ray 8E
Earl, Jack 7
East Cambridge, Massachusetts 8B
East Liverpool Potteries Co. 8B
Eastwood-Park Co. 8E
Eaton, Moses 7
Eaton, William 8E
Eaves & Herbel 8E
EA. & W. Mfg. Co. 8E
E.B. 2, 8E
E.B. & C. 2
Eberlein, Johann Friedrich 2
Eberly, J., & Bro. 8B
Ebner, David 7
Echizen Kinai School 2
Eckart, G. 8E
Eckert, Horst 2
Eckhardt Bros. 2
Eckstein & Richardson 8E
Ecuadorian Panama Hat Co. 8D
E. Cvcci 8D
E.D. 8E
Eddi 8D
Edgar, P., & Son 8E
Edinburgh 8B
Edkins, Michael 2
Edmands, Barnabas 8E
Edmands & Co. 8B
Edmond & Co. 8E
Edmonds, Nelson 8N
Edmond's Pottery 8B
Edmonds, W.G., & Co. 8E
Edo-Hirata School 2
Edwards, John 8B, 8E
Edwards, Jonathan 8E
Edwards, Joseph, Jr. 8E
Edwards, Samuel 8E

Edwards, Thomas 8E
E.E. 8E
Ees, Garrit 2
E.F. 2, 8B
Eggington Rich Glass Co.
    8B
Eggleston, Jacob 8E
Ehrmann, Eugene 2
Eiji 2
Eisch, Erwin 8B
Eiseman & Co. 8D
Eiseman, Florence 8D
Eisenberg & Sons 8D
Eisenbrant, C. H. 8N
Eisenhut 8E
E. & J.B. 8B
E.J.P. Co. 8E
E.L.B. 2
Elberg, Henry H. 8C
Eleder-Hickok Co. 8E
Elers, John P. & David 8B
Eley, William 8E
Eley, William, & Fearn,
    William 8E
Elgin American Mfg. Co.
    8E
Elkhart Band Instrument
    Co. 8N
Elkin, Knight & Bridg-
    wood 8B
Ellerby 8E
Elliot 8D
Ellis, Jackson, Co. 2
Ellry, H.L. 8B
Elmer, Don 2
Elmslie, George Grant 2, 7
E.L.S. 2
Elson & Wolf 8E
Elsworth, William 8E
E.M. 2
Emery, Stephen 8E
Emes, John 8E
Emme Boutique 8D
Emmons, L. 8E
Empire Pottery 8B
Enfield Pottery & Tile
    Works 2
Engel-Fetzer 8D
Engelhardt, V. 2
Engstrom, Robert 2
Enterprise Cut Glass Co.
    8B
Eoff & Moore 8E
E.P. 8E
E.R. 8B
Erard Freres & Co. 8N
Erard, Sebastian 8N

Erat, P. 8N
Erben, Henry 8N
Ericson & Weiss 2
Eriksen, Sigurd Alf. 2
Erlebacher 8D
Ernest, William H. 8B
Ernst 8E
Erskine, Alice 2
Erwin & Dugdale 8C
Erwin, H. 8E
Erwin, Hobart 2
Eschenbach, G. 8N
Esherick, Wharton 7
E.S.T. 8E
Este 8D
Estevez 8D
Estey 8N
Estey, New Mexico 8B
Etcheverry, Louisa 2
Etruria 2
Etts, Richard 2
Euler 8N
Evan-Picone 8D
Evans 2
Evans, Alfred R. 8B
Evans, D., & Co. 2
Evans, Dick 7
Evans, Robert 8E
Evans, T., & Co. 8E
Evans, Timothy 7
Evette & Schaeffer 8N
Evins, David 8D
E.W. 8E
E.W. & G. 8E
Exeter Pottery Works 8B
Expanso 8D
Exquisite Form 8D
EZ 8D

F. 2
Faber, A.W. 2
Fabius & Corago 8B
Fagan 8N
Fager, Charles 7
Fahrenheitor 2
Faience Mfg. Co. 8B
Fairbanks, E.T., & Co. 8E
Fairbanks, J. 8E
Fairy 8D
Fairyland 8D
Falconet, Etienne-Maurice
    2
Falconetto Designs 2
Fales, I. 8E
Famous Barr Co. 8D
Fanning 8C
Farnham, Henry 8E

Farrar, Caleb 8B
Farrar, Isaac Brown 8B
Farrington & Hunnewell
    8E
Fassler, A. 2
Fasson & Sons 8E
Fast, Ralph R. 8B
Fath, Jacques 8D
Faubourg Saint-Denis 2
Fauchier Factory 2
Faucon, E. 2
Fau & Guillard 2
Faul, Henry 8B
Faulkner 2
Fauveau 8E
Favre, C. 2
Fawdery, William 2
Fawn's Fashions 8D
Faye Creations 8D
F. & B. 8D
F.B. 8E
F.C. 8B
Fearn, William, & Eley,
    William 8E
Federal Glass Co. 8B
Feder, Edith M. 2
Federhen, John, Jr. 8E
Federici, Amanda 8S
Feldenheimer, A. 8E
Feldhar, Gerhardt 8N
Feldman, Beverly 8D
Feliu 8N
Felten, Frances 7
Fench & Koom 8D
Fenicchia, Concetta 7
Fennell, Edith 8E
Fenton Art Glass Co. 8B
Fenton Bros. 8E
Fenton, Christopher Web-
    ber 8B
Fenton & Hancock 8B
Fenton, J. 8B
Fenton, Jacob 8B
Fenton, Jonathan 8B
Fenton, Leander 8B
Fenton, Richard Lucas 8B
Ferber, Lee 7
Fereday, Thomas 2
Ferguson, Ken 8B
Ferguson 8D
Fermanagh 8B
Feron, Louis 2
Fessenden Bros. 8E
Feu, J. 2
Feves, Betty W. 8B
F.F. 2, 8E
F.G.B. 8E

Gabler, E., & Bros. 8N
Gaby, Nina 7
Gaffney, James D. 2
Gaffney, Nelly 8D
Gagliano, Joseph, Nico-
laus, & Januarius 8N
Gaillard, P. 8N
Gainesborough 8D
Galanga 8D
Galanos 8D
Gala, S.F. 8E
Gale & Hayden 8E
Gale, J. 8E
Gale, William, & Son 8E
Gale & Willis 8E
Gale, Wood & Hughes 8E
Galland, Pierre-Victor 2
Gallant, Frank 8D
Gallant, Frank, Co. 8D
Gallatin, Albert 8B
Galle, Andre 2
Galle, Emile 2, 8B, 8E
Galley, Merritt 8N
Galligan, William J. 2
Galligan, William J., Inc. 2
Galligan, William J., &
Sons Corp. 2
Galligan, W.J., & Sons 2
Galluba & Hofmann 8B
Galpin, Rev. F.W. 8N
Galt, M.W., & Bro. 8E
Galt, M.W., Bro. & Co. 8E
Gambault 8E
Gambon, A. 8N
Ganer, Christopher 8N
Gano Downs 8D
Gant Madeleine 8D
Ganter & Mattern Co. 8D
Gardiner 8E
Gardiner, B. 8E
Gardiner, Baldwin 2
Gardner & Co. 8E
Gardner, Floyd A. 8N
Gardner, Francis 8B
Gardner, Joseph 8B
Gardner, May C. 8D
Gardner's 8B
Garfinckel & Siegel 8D
Garfinkel, Julius, & Co.
8D
Garner 8B
Garnier, P. 2
Garrett, Philip 8E
Garrine Lacroix 8D
G.A.S. 8E
Gaskel & Chambers 8E
Gaspart 8D

Gates 8E
Gates, Louisa 8S
Gates Potteries 8B
Gatewood, Fannie 8S
Gatteaux, E. 2
Gatteaux, Jacques-
Edouard 2
Gatteaux, Nicolas M. 2
Gaul, John F. 8E
Gautier, Henri 8N
Gautrot Aine 8N
Gautrot-Marquet 8N
Gavioli & Cie 8N
Gavotte, a la 8D
Gaynes, Coral W. 2
Gayrard, Raymond 2
Gazal 2
Gazetta, C. 8E
G. & B. 2
G.B. 8E
G.C. 8E
G. & Cie 2
G.C.N. 8N
G.D. 8E
GDA 7
Geddes, James 8E
Geddes & Stewart 8E
Geffroy, C.H.H. 2
Geib 8N
Geib, John, & Son 8N
Geib, William 8N
Geismar, Hermann 2
Geismar, Suzanne 2
Gelston, Hugh 8E
Gelston & Treadwell 8E
General Electric Co. 2
Genesee Silver Plate 8E
Genest 8B
Gennaro, Giovanni Bat-
tista 8N
Geoffroy & Co. 8B
Gera 2
Gerardin & Watson 8E
Gerhardt, G. 8E
Gernreich, Rudi 8D
Gerock 8N
Gertz 8D
Gessendo 2
Gethen, J.W. 8E
Getzen 8N
Getz, John 8E
Gevilly 2
G.G. 8E
G.H.B. Co. 8E
Giampietro, Alexander 8B
Giano Knits 8D
Gibbons, Edward 8E

Gibbons, Grinling 2
Gibbons, John 2
Gibbs, John 8E
Gibney, M. 8E
Gibson, Charles Dana 2
Gibson & Davis 8N
Gibson, Edward 8B
Gibson Guitar & Man-
dolin Co. 8N
Gien 2, 8B
Giffen, Thomas, & Town-
send, John 8E
Gifford, C.E., & Co. 2
Gilbert 8D
Gilbert, F.S. 8E
Gilbert, Lemuel 8N
Gilbert, Timothy, & Co.
8N
Gilbert, W. 8E
Gilden, Jeny 8D
Giles, George 8E
Gilhooly, David 7
Gille, Jne. 8B
Gilleland 8B
Gillet & Fils 2
Gillinder & Bennett 8B
Gillinder, James, & Sons
8B
Gillinder & Sons 8B
Gillispie 8E
Gill, John H. 8B
Gill, William 8B
Gimbel Bros. 8D
Gimbel's 8D
Ginori 8B, 8D
Giovannozzi, Ottaviano
8B
G.I.P. 2
Girl Graduate Registered
8D
Gist, Mary Stirrett 8S
Givenchy, Hubert 8C, 8D
G.J. / D.F. 8E
G.K. 2, 8E
G.L. 8E
Glamorgan Pottery 8B
Glascock Mfg. Co. 8E
Glasgow Pottery Co. 7, 8B
Glass, Peter 8E
Glass Tubes & Compo-
nents, Ltd. 8B
Gleason, Roswell 8E
Giebe Street Works 8B
Gledhill Wall Paper Co. 2
Glencraft 2
Glencraft Adelphi Impe-
rial 2

Glendenning, J. 8C
Glen Haven 8D
Glidden Pottery 8B
Glier, M. 8N
Gloria Knitwear 8D
G.M.J. 8E
Gobb 8D
Goberis, Theodora C.T. 2
Goddu, Louis 8D
Godfroy, Clair 8N
Goins, Luther 8C
Gold Bond 8D
Goldring, J. 8E
Goldstein, I. 8E
Goldt, Jacobus Heinrich
8N
Goldworm 8D
Golfe-Juan 8B
Goltzius, Julius 2
Gonzalez, Hijos de 8N
Goodale, Daniel, Jr. 8B
Goodale & Stedman 8B
Goodhue 8E
Goodhue, John 8E
Goodrich, B.F. 8D
Goodrich, Eben 8N
Goodridge, Joseph 8D
Goodsell, W.J. 8E
Goodwin Bros. 8B
Goodwin, Horace 8B, 8E
Goodyear 2, 8D
Goo, Gwen-Lin 7
Goran, Gerd 2
Gordon 800 8D
Gordon & Ferguson 8D
Gordon, G. 8E
Gordon, R. & G. 8B
Gorgas, S. 8E
Gorham Co. 2, 7, 8E
Gorham & Co. 8E
Gorham Co. Founders 2
Gorham Corp. 8E
Gorham, J., & Son 8E
Gorham Mfg. Co. 2, 7,
8D, 8E
Gorham Silver Co. 8E
Gorham & Webster 8E
Gorman 8D
Gorozayemon Tomonobu
2
Gossamer 8D
Goteborg Tapetfabrik 2
Gotha 2, 8B
Goto Hachirobei 2
Goto Hachirobei Kwanjo 2
Goto Hachirobei School 2
Goto Hanzayemon 2

Goto Hanzayemon School
2
Goto Hojo, Mitsuaki 2
Goto Ichijo 2
Goto, Ichijo School 2
Goto Jujo 2
Goto Kijo 2
Goto Mitsubumi 2
Goto Mitsumasa 2
Goto Renjo 2
Goto Rihei School 2
Goto School 2
Goto Seijo Rokudai 2
Goto Seijo School 2
Goto Shinjo 2
Goto Shirobei School 2
Goto Shunjo 2
Goto Tokujo 2
Gotz, Gottfried Bernhard
2
Gougan, Jean 8B
Goulding & Co. 8N
Goulding, E.H. 8E
Gouthiere 2
Gouthiere, Pierre 2
Goz, Johann 2
G.P. 8E
G.R. 2, 8B
GR. 2
Grace, The 8D
Graf, Philip, Wallpapers
Inc. 2
Gragg, Samuel 8E
Graham, Anna Krohn 2
Granada 8B
Grandjean, Caroline F. 2
Granger, Joseph 8S
Granger, Mrs. Joseph 8S
Grant 8D
Grant, G.H. 8C
Grant, W.T. 8D
Gras, Georges 8E
Grassi 8N
Grauel, D. 8E
Graves Co. 2
Graves & Co. 8N
Graves, Robert, Co. 2
Gray 8B, 8D
Gray, Robert 8E
Gray, Robert & William
8N
Greaves, W., & Sons 8E
Greco, N. 8D
Greely & Morrill 2
Green, Daniel, Felt Shoe
Co. 8D
Green, Guy 2

Green, John M. 8E
Green, Kenneth 2
Green, Michael J.W. 2
Green, Samuel 8E
Greensburg 8B
Greenwood, M., & Co. 8E
Greenwood Pottery Co.
8B
Greer, Howard 8D
Greff Fabrics, Inc. 2
Gregg, Thomas 8C
Gregory, John 2
Gregory, Samuel 8E
Gregory, Waylande 7
Grenelle 8D
Grenser, Heinrich 8N
Grey, Hannah 8S
Gricci, Felipe 2
Griesling & Schlott 8N
Griffen, Smith & Hill 8B
Griffith, Robert 7
Grimmer 2
Grinderiz 8B
Grindley 8B
Grindley, W. H., & Co. 7
Grinty Hotel Ware 8B
Grinwalt, Johann 8N
Griswold, Ashbil 8E
Grosjean & Woodward 8E
Grosner's 8D
Grossman, James 8N
Grotell, Maija 2, 8B
Groult, Andre 2
Grove, D.B. 8N
Grubb, Nils 2
Grubb, Olof 2
Grueby Faience Co. 2, 8B
Gruppe 2
G.U. 8E
Gubbio 2
Gucci 8D
Guerin, William & Co. 7
Guerlain, Pierre 2
Gueyton, Alexander 8E
Gugelot, Hans 2
Guiliano, Carlo 2
Guimard, Adeline Op-
penheim 2
Guimard, Hector 2
Gunther Jaeckel 8D
Gurrier, Elizabeth 7
Gustavsberg 2
Gutman, Julius, & Co. 8E
Guyot, Charles 8D
G.V. 8E
G. & W. 8E
G.W. 8E

G.W.C. 8E
Gyorky, Aranka 8D

H. 8D, 8E
H.A.?. 2
H.A. 8E
Haband Co. 8D
Haberacker, John 8N
Hache et Pepin a Paris 8B
Hache, Julien, & Co. 8B
Hachido School 2
Hackle, William 8E
Hackwood, William 8B
Hadfield, A. 8E
Hadley 8D
Hadley, James 2
H.A./ E.A./ F.A. 8E
Haeger Potteries 8B
Haerdtl, Osvald 2
Haggerty, J.J. 8D
Hagiua Shohei, Katsuhira
   2
Hagiya School 2
Hagstrum Bros. 8D
Haig 8B
Haight, Nelson 8E
Haig, James & Thomas 8B
Haines, Frank & Elizabeth
   2
Halari 8N
Hald, Edward 2, 8B
Haldy, F.P. 8D
Hale 8N
Hall 8N
Hallay 8B
Hall, Doris 2
Hall & Elton 8E
Hall's Fazar Form Co. 8D
Hall, William 8B
Hall, William, & Son 8N
Halpern, Lea 8B
Halston 8D
Halvorsen, Liza 7
Hamada, Shoji 8B
Hamano Masayuki 2
Hamano Naoyuki 2
Hamano Noriyuki 2
Hamano School 2
Hamano Shozui 2
Hamber, W. 8N
Hamburger, Isaac, & Sons
   8D
Hamersley, Thomas 8E
Hamilton, James 8B
Hamilton, James, & Co.
   8B
Hamilton & Jones 8B

Hamilton Mfg. Co. 8E
Hamilton Road Pottery 8B
Hamlin 8N
Hamlin, Samuel 8E
Hamlin, Samuel E., Jr. 8E
Hamlin, William 8E
Hammersley & Co. 8B
Hammond Instrument
   Co. 8N
Hammond Organ Co. 8N
Hampden Park 8D
Hampshire Pottery 8B
Hancock, Robert 7
Handa Belts 8D
Handex Corp. 7
Handmacher 8D
Hanel, Jules, & Co. 8D
Hannaford 8E
Hanners, George 8E
Hannong, Joseph 2
Hansen, Carl 8N
Hansen 8D
Hansen, E. 2
Hanshu 2
Han-Tec 2
Hapgood, J. 8B
Harben Papers, Inc. 2
Harbeson, Benjamin 8E
Harden, John M. 8B
Harden, Thomas 8B
Harder, Charles 8B
Harding, Newell 8E
Harker, Taylor, & Co. 8B
Harland, Thomas 8E
Harlan, Ethel I. 2
Harley, G. 8E
Harman & Co. 2
Haroni Inc. 8D
Harper & Fagan 8N
Harper, John 8N
Harrington, Thompson 8B
Harris, D. Walter 8D
Harris, M. 8D
Harrison, C.P. 8E
Harrison, J. 8E
Harrison, John 8D
Harrison, Louise 8S
Harris Raincoat Co. 8D
Hart 8E
Hart, J.C. 8D
Hartman, Philip 8E
Hart, Schaffner & Marx
   8D
Hart Sensible Shoes 8D
Harty, M. Fillmore 7
Haruaki Hogen 2
Haruhide 2

Haruteru 2
Haruyuki 2
Hashimoto Ikkin 2
Hashimoto Ikkin School 2
Hashimoto School 2
Hasler, John 8N
Haspel 8D
Hastier, John 8E
Hastings, G.G. 8N
Hastings, Wellington 8B
Hastrick 8N
Hata Nobuyoshi 2
Hathaway 8D
Hauten, H. 2
Havard, Lecellier 8E
Havet, Mme. 8D
Haviland, Charles Field 2
Haviland & Co. 2, 7, 8B
Haviland, Theodore 8B
Haviland, Theodore, &
   Co. 7
Havone 8E
Hawkes, T.G., & Co. 8B
Hawking, Clarence 2
Hawkins, John Isaac 8N
Hawks, Julia A. 8S
Hawksworth, Eyre & Co.,
   Ltd. 8E
Hawley Bros. 8B
Hawmes 8E
Haxstun, Andrew K. 8B
Hayden, Audrey C. 8B
Hayden & Gregg 8E
Hayd, Eustach 2
Hayer, Robert & ? 2
Hayes & Adriance 8E
Hayes, P.P. 8E
Haymaker 8D
Hayner, E. 8C
Haynes, Bennett Co. 8B
Haynes, D.F., & Co. 8B
Hayt, Babcock & Apple-
   ton 8N
Hayward & Son 2
Hazel Atlas Glass Co. 8B
Hazen 8E
H.B. 8E
H.D. 8E
H.E. 8E
Healey, Ned 8D
Health-Tex 8D
Healy 8N
Heath, Henry, Ltd. 8D
Heaton, Maurice 2
Heberlin 2
Hedberg, Lars 2
Heianjo School 2

Ka Kwong Hui 2
Kalflex 2
Kamakura School 2
Kamayama School 2
Kambei Goto School 2
Kami Yoshi School 2
Kandler, Johann Joachim 2
Kaneharu 2
Kaneiye 2
Kaneiye III 2
Kaneiye School 2
Kanewaka 2
Kann Bros. Silver Co. 8E
Kanns, S., Sons Co. 8D
Kano Natsuo 2
Kaolin Porcelain Works 8B
Karasz, Ilonka 2
Karfiol, Bernard 2
Karhula-Iittala 2
Karina, Elena 7
Karlby, Bent 2
Karp, J. 8E
Karr, Albert H. 8N
Kashan 2
Kaskel & Kaskel 8D
Kasper 8D
Kasper for J.L. Sport, Ltd.
 8D
Kasper of Arnold Fox 8D
Kassel Werk Akademie 2
Kasson 8D
Kasuga School 2
Katataka 2
Katchu, Miochin School 2
Katchushi 2
Katchushi School 2
Katchusi 2
Katsufusa 2
Katsuhira 2
Katsuki School 2
Katzenbach & Warren 8E
Katzenbach & Warren,
 Inc. 2
Kaufmann's 8D
Kave, J. 8E
Kawabayashi School 2
Kawaji School 2
Kawarabayashi Hidekune
 2
Kaye, Ellen 8D
Kayser 8D
Kayser, Engelbert 2, 7
Kayser, Frederick A. 2
Kayser, J.P., & Sons 7
Kayser, R., Clothing Mfg.
 8D
Kayserzinn 7

Kazarichi Rihachi 2
Kazunori 2
K.E. 8E
Kean, James 8D
Kearsing, John, & Sons
 8N
Keds 8D
Keeler, Joseph 8E
Keene 8E
Keene, New Hampshire
 8B
Keeney, A. 8E
Kees, Ernst, Fabrique 8D
Keily 8B
Keister, Amos 8B
Keister, J., & Co. 8B
Keister, Jeremiah 8B
Keller 8N
Keller, Dan 8D
Keller, Georg 2
Kellerman, Margaret 2
Kelley & Moore 8D
Kellogg, S. 8E
Kelly, Frank Reuss 2
Kelly, J. 8E
Kelty, Alexander 8E
Kemble, James, Mills Inc.
 2
Kempe, Margot 2
Kendall, Loammi 8B
Kenjo Hachirobei Goto 2
Kenriushi Nagayoshi 2
Kensington Glass Works
 8B
Kent, John 7
Kenton Hills Porcelains 8B
Kenusai Naotoshi 2
Keramic Art Works 8B
Kerner, I. 8N
Kern, P.E. 8E
Kerns, J.F. 8C
Kerr, William B., & Co.
 8D, 8E
Ketcham & Mc Dougall
 8D
Keyser Bros. Metal Work-
 ers 8E
Key, Thomas 8N
Keyworth, Robert 8E
Kidd, I. 8E
Kiedolps, F. 8N
Kieffer, C. 8E
Kien, Yanagisawa 7
Kikuchi School 2
Kikugawa School 2
Kiku Muneyoshi 2
Kikuoka School 2

Kilgour, French & Stan-
 bury, Ltd. 8D
Kilguss, George J., &
 Bros. 8E
Kilner, John 8B
Kimball, J. 8E
Kimball, John 8E
Kimball, Leverett 8E
Kimbel & Cabus 8E
Kimberly Knitwear 8D
Kim, Ernie 8B
Kinai School 2
King, M.W. 8E
King, R. 8E
Kingsbury-Sweetland,
 Electa 8S
Kington, Louis Brent 7
Kinora Co., Ltd 2
Kinsey 8E
Kinsey, Edward 8E
Kinsey, Edward & David
 8E
Kinyemon Rioye 2
Kioto Kinko 2
Kioto School 2
Kirby, William 8E
Kirchhain 2
Kirchner, Johann Gottlob
 2
Kirckman, Jacobus &
 Abraham 8N
Kirkman & Son 8N
Kirkpatrick, Cornwall &
 Wallace 8B
Kirk, Samuel 2, 8E
Kirk, Samuel, & Son 2, 8E
Kirk, Samuel, & Sons 7
Kirk, S., & Son Co. 8E
Kirk, S., & Son, Inc. 8E
Kiseljak, Bosnia 8B
Kishi Masayoshi 2
Kisting, H., & Sons 8N
Kitts 8E
Kitts, John, & Co. 8E
Kiukodo Hiroyuki 2
Kiyu 2
Klappman Freres 8N
Klee Bros. & Co. 8D
Klein, Anne, & Co. 8D
Klein, Calvin 8D
Kleinert's 8D
Klemm 8N
Klemm & Bros. 8N
Klingling, Johann George
 2
Kloss, John 8D
Kloster-Veilsdorf 8B

Marsh, Edwin Thomas 8B
Marsh, Jordan, Co. 8D
Marteau, Francois-Joseph
 2
Marteney, Eugene 8N
Martin 8E
Martin-Baron 2
Martin Bros. 8N
Martin, C.F. 8N
Martinez, Apolonio O. 8C
Martinez, Julian 7
Martinez, Maria 7
Martinez, Santana 7
Martin, Hall & Co., Ltd.
 8E
Martin, Jean Francois 8N
Martin, Joe 2
Martin, May 8S
Martin, Pollman & Co. 8N
Martz, Karl 8B
Marum, Lawrence 8N
Marvay 8D
Masa 2
Masaaki I 2
Masafusa 2
Masakata 2
Masamitsu 2
Masamitsu Yedo 2
Masamoto Naosaki 2
Masanao 2
Masanobu 2
Masanobu Yasuda 2
Masaoka Minayama 2
Masatada 2
Masatoshi 2
Masatoyo 2
Masatsugu 2
Masatsune 2
Masayoshi 2
Masayuki 2
Mashiko Masayuki 2
Mason 2
Mason, Bertha 2
Mason, George Miles 8B
Mason & Hamlin 8N
Mason, Harry, Ltd. 8E
Masriera Y Caneras 2
Masson, Jean-August 2
Mather, Fred 8N
Mathews, Richard 8E
Matisse, Henri 2
Matson, Newell 8E
Matsuteru 2
Matta 2
Matthews 8D
Maubossin Workshop 7
Mauger, Jean 2

Maw & Co. 8B
Maximilian, Mme. Potok
 of 8D
Maxwell, S.A., & Co. 2
Maxwell, Vera 8D
Mayer 8D
Mayer, Elijah 8B
Mayer, J. 8B
Mayer Pottery 8B
Maynard, C. 8E
Maynard & Taylor 8E
Mayr, Sebastian 8N
Mayse, John 8N
May, The 8D
M.C. 2, 8E
M.C.A. & Co. 2
M. de E. 2
Meacham, George W. 8E
Meacham & Pond 8N
Mead & Adriance 8E
Mead, E., & Co. 8E
Meaders, Mrs. Cheever
 8B
Mead, John O., & Sons 8E
Meakin, Charles 8B
Meakin, J. & G. 8B
Mealey, John 8C
Mechanics Sterling Co. 8E
Medalist Industries 8C
Medaris, Millie 8S
Meeks, Edward 8E
Megear, Thomas J. 8E
Meggers, Bertha Bork 8S
Mehetable, Martha 8S
Meier 8D
Meigh, Charles 8B
Meinl & Lauber 8N
Meis, B. 8E
Meissen 2, 8B
Meissioner, C. 8E
Meizan Yabu 2
Melbourne Pottery 8B
Melendandri, R. 8D
Meller, Mellerio Dits 7
Mellon, Sarah Ann 8S
Mellor, Venables, & Co.
 8B
Melo-Pean Co. 8N
Melotti, Fausto 2
Melton, Jacob 8N
Melville, David 8E
Melville, Thomas 8E
Menard & Burghard 8E
Mendel, M. 8D
Mendler 8N
Mene, P.J. 2
Menkins 8E

Mennecy 2, 8B
Mennecy-Villeroy 2
Mensch, Pieter Simon 8B
Mercer Pottery Co. 8B
Mercer, William R. 2
Merchant, Weldon 7
Meredith 8N
Meriden Britannia Co. 8E
Meriden Co. 2
Meriden Cutlery Co. 8E
Meriden Silver Plate Co.
 7, 8E
Mermod Freres 8N
Mermod & Jaccard 8E
Mermod, Jaccard & King
 Co. 8E
Merola 8D
Merrimac Hat Corp. 8D
Merrimac Pottery 8B
Merriman, Samuel 8E
Merritt, Ira 8D
Mersick, Edwin E. 8E
Mertoli 2
Merton 8D
Merz, H. 8C
Metzler 8N
Meuber, H. 8D
Meuber, Marcus 8D
Meyer, Conrad 8N
Meyer, Friedrich Elias 2
Meyer, Henry 8E
Meyer, H.F. 8N
M.M. 8B, 8E
M.M. Co. 8E
Moba 2
Mobi Corp. 7
Mobile 8B
Mochica Culture (Peru) 2
Modella 8D
Modern Juniors 8D
Modern Miss 8D
Modic, Mary 8S
Modura Poterie 2
Moeur, Mrs. B.B. 8S
Mohamed, Ethel W. 7
Moholy-Nagy, Lazlo 2
Moir, J. & W. 8E
M.O.L. 8B
Molander, Harold 2
Molded Fiberglass Tray
 Co. 2
Moldenhawer, Hammer 2
Molineux, George, & Ca-
 pen, Ephraim 8E
Molineux, John 8E
Moller, C. 2
Moller, H. 8E

Peoria Pottery Co. 8B
Pepper, H.J. 8E
Pepper, J.W., & Son 8N
Perchellet, L. 8D
Perdriaux, P.G. 8E
Peretti, Elsa 2
Perfectionne C T 2
Perfectionne E B 2
Perfectionne E L 2
Perfectionne L C B 2
Perfect Knit Togs 8D
Per Fetex 8D
Perier, Casimir 8B
Perinet, F. 8N
Perkins, G.F. 8C
Perkins, J. 8E
Perley, Charles 8C
Perley, Charles A. 8E
Perma, Pat 8D
Perrier, Rue du Back 54 8B
Perrin, La Veuve 2, 8B
Perron, Ph. 2
Perrot, Bernard 2
Perrotta, Joseph 8C
Perry & Co. 8D, 8E
Perry, Mary Chase 8B
Perry, Richard 8N
Pesce, Gaetano 7
Peter Pan 8D
Petit & du Perier 2
Petit, Jacob 8B
Petit, Louis-Michel 2
Pettersen, Mathias 2
Petti 8D
Pettibone Mfg. Co. 2
Pettingill & Pear 8E
Pewabic Pottery 8B
P.F. ? 2
Pfaff, John 8N
Pfeiffer, Carl A. 8N
Pfeuffer, Christoph Karl 2
P.G. 8E, 8N
P.G.L. 2
Philadelphia, Pennsylvania 8B
Philmaid 8D
P.H.L. 2
Phl 2
Phoenix Clothes 8D
Phoenix Glass Co. 8B
Phoenixville, Chester Co., Pennsylvania 8B
Pianola, U.S.A. 8N
Piatto, Franciscus de 8N
Piazza Prints, Inc. 2
Picasso, Pablo 2
Pieces 8D

Piehl, J.H. 8C
Pierce, Samuel 8E
Pierce, William 8N
Piercy, Henry 8B
Pierre, G. 8E
Pierret 2
Piggott, Francis 8E
Pignet, Auguste, et Fils 2
Pilgrim Swimwear 8D
Pilot 8D
Pine, Mrs. Platt S. 8S
Pinet, F. 8D
Pingat, E. 8D
Pingret, Arnould-Joseph 2
Pinxton 8B
Pinzeci, Persinger 8N
Pippin, Eugenia 8S
Pisgah Forest Pottery 8B
Pitkin 8E
Pitman, Saunders 8E
Pitteroff, G.C. 2
Pittman, Aaron 8C
Pittsburgh, Pennsylvania 8B
Pittsburgh W-P Co. 2
Pitts, William 2
P.K.Z. 8D
P.L. 8E
Pla, Josefina 8B
Plako 8D
Plane Porcelain Factory 8B
Plant, J.H. 8B
Plant, Prof. J.B. 8D
Plastic Ware, Inc. 2
Platner, Warren 2
Platt, A.H. 8E
Player, Johannes 8N
Playtex 8D
Plaza South 8D
Plazvid 2
Ples, Adolphe 8N
Plesber, Francesco 8N
Plesbler 8N
Pleyel 8N
Plimpton, James L. 8C
Plummer, William 2, 8E
Pluvinet, L.M. 2
Plymouth 8B, 8D
P.M. 8E
P.M.I. Corp. 8N
Poillon Pottery 8B
Pointons 8B
Poiret 8D
Poiret, Paul 8D
Poli, Flavio 2
Pollard, Donald 2
Pollard, William 8E

Pollock, Benjamin 2
Polly Flinders 8D
Polo 8D
Pommer, Charles 8N
Pond 8N
Pons 8N
Pont-aux-Choux 2, 8B
Poole, Julia A. 8S
Poole Silver Co. 8E
Poor 8E
Pope Gosser China Co. 8B
Popov Factory 8B
Porcelaine de la Reine 8B
Porcelaine de Paris 8B
Porter, F.W. 8E
Porter, James 8E
Porter, N. 8D
Portland Glass Co. 8B
Portland Stoneware Co. 8B
Portobello 8B
Port Richmond Pottery 8B
Posey, Frederick J. 8E
Positano 2
Possony, Vally 8B
Postawka, Louis 8E
Post, George B. 8E
Potok, Charlotte 7
Potok, Mme. 8D
Potrel, Moos 2
Potschappel 8B
Potsdam 8B
Potter 8N
Potter, Alvin 8N
Potter, C. & J.G. 2
Potter, J.O. 8E
Potter, Lewis & Co. 8E
Potthast Bros. 8E
Pottier & Stymus 8B
Poulsen, O. 8E
Pourcelle, Henry 8N
Poussin, S. 2
Pouyat, J. 7
Powell & Bishop 8B
Powell, Mrs. Fielding Travis 8S
Powell, W. 8E
Powers, Harriet 8S
Powolny, Michael 2
P.R. 2, 8E
Prange, Sally Bowen 7
Pratt, F. & R., & Co. 8B
Pratt, William, & Bro. 8E
Precheur, Baron 8D
Precoisa 8D
Preiss 2
Prema, Pat 8D

Wackerle, Joseph 2
Wadhams, A. Elizabeth 2
Wagan, R.M., & Co. 2
Wagner, Thomas S. 2
Wait, Luke & Obediah 8B
Waitzkin, Stella 7
Walcott, Mary L. 8S
Waldhauser, George 8N
Waldman 8D
Waldman, Joseph 8B
Walenta, E.J. 2
Wales, Bettie 2
Wales, Betty 8D
Wales Goodyear Shoe Co. 8D
Walker, Knowles & Co. 8E
Walker, Thomas B. 8N
Walker, William 8C
Walk Over 8D
Wallace 8E
Wallace, R., & Sons Mfg. Co. 8D, 8E
Wall, Dr. 8B
Wallendorf 2, 8B
Walley, William J. 8B
Wallis, Thomas 8E
Wallpaper Manufacturers Ltd. 2
Wall Trends, Inc. 2
Walters, Carl 7
Waltham Co. 8D
Walton 2
Walton, John 8B, 8E
Wamsley, Mrs. 8D
Wanamaker, John 8D
Ward 2
Ward, Louise 8S
Ward's Wallpaper & Paint 2
Warford, Joseph 8E
Warner 8E
Warner, AL. & C.A. 8E
Warner, Andrew E. 8E
Warner, Caleb 8E
Warner Co. 2
Warner, H. 8E
Warner's 8D
Warner, T. 8E
Warner, Thomas 8E
Warne, Thomas 8B
Warren's 8D
Warren's Featherbone 8D
Warren, Thomas E. 8E
Warwick China Co. 8B
Warwick Pottery 8B
Warwick Sterling Co. 8E
Washburn Co. 8N

Washburn, George 8N
Wasson, H.P., Co. 8D
Waterbury Brass Co. 8E
Waterbury Button Co. 2
Waterford 2, 8B
Waterman, Nathaniel, Jr. 8E
Waterman, Sabra 8E
Waters, Beatrice 2
Watkins, C.M. 8B
Watkins, Joan P. 8B
Watkins, J.Y. 8E
Watkins, J.Y., & Son 8E
Watling Mfg. Co. 8C
Watrous Mfg. Co. 8E
Watson 8E
Watson Co. 8D, 8E
Watson, Edward 8E
Watson Foster Co. 2
Watson, James 8E
Watson, Thomas 8E
Watts, Benjamin 8E
Waugh, Sidney 8B
W.B. 8E
W.C. 8E
W.D. 8E
W.D./ C. 8E
W.E. 8E
Weathervane Handmacher 8D
Weaver, James L. 8B
Weaver, T. 8C
Webb 8E
Webb, Joseph 8E
Webb, Thomas, & Sons 2, 8B
Webb, William Holmes 8E
Weber 7
Webster Co. 8E
Webster, E.G., & Son 7, 8E
Webster, H.L., & Co. 8E
Webster, Mack C. 8B
Wedgwood 2, 7
Wedgwood & Bentley 2, 8B
Wedgwood & Co. 8B
Wedgwood, Josiah 8B
Wedgwood, Josiah, & Co. 8B
Wedgwood, Josiah, & Sons 2
Wednesbury 2
Weeks, Elizabeth 8S
Wegely, Wilhelm Kaspar 8B
Wegner, Hans J. 2

Weidemeyer, J.M. 8E
Weigall, Charles Harvey 2
Weinerger 8D
Weingarten 8D
Weingartner, J. 8E
Weisse, I.W. 8N
Weitzel, Jacob 8E
Weitz, John 8D
Welch, Margetson, & Co., Ltd. 8D
Welk, E. 2
Weller, Samuel A., Pottery 8B
Welles 8E
Welling, William 8D
Wells, David D. 8B
Wells, Isaac N. 8B
Wellsville China Co. 8B
Welsh, Henry D. 8S
Welter, P. 8E
Wembley 8D
Wescott, Paul 2
Weser Bros. 8N
West 8D
West, Betty 8S
Westbury Fashions 8D
Western Stoneware Co. 8B
Westford, Connecticut 8B
Westinghouse 8D
West, James 8E
Westmore Bros. 8C
Westmoreland Glass Co. 8B
Westmoreland Specialty Co. 8B
Weston Priory 8B
West Troy Pottery 8B
Wettach, A.G. 2
W.E./ W.F. 8E
Wexler, Peter 2
Weygandt, Thomas J. 8N
W.F. 8E
W.H. 2, 8E
W. & H. 8E
Whaites & Charters 8N
W. & H. Co. 8E
Wheat, Esther 8S
Wheeler, Stuart 2
Wheeling Pottery Co. 8B
Whelen 8D
Whieldon, Thomas 2, 8B
Whipham, Thomas 8E
Whisler, Matilda Kramer 8S
Whitall, Tatum Factory 2, 8B